P9-CKD-502

Life *is* a trip. Judith Fein's globetrotting adventures remind us that we travel to be changed, in big ways and small. This book is immensely readable, steeped in a spirit of connecting with place, with each other, and with our inner selves. Get a massage in Vietnam, travel the land of the witches, and meet a joyous rabbi. You're in the hands of a writer who has a keen eye and a singular voice.

Keith Bellows, Editor-in-Chief, National Geographic Traveler

I don't travel unless I have to. I don't know Micronesia from a microwave. In fact, I find it annoying just to walk from one end of my tiny bungalow to the other, yet when I read Judith Fein's incredible new book, *Life Is A Trip: The Transformative Magic of Travel*, I found myself eagerly tagging along on one adventure after another. Ms. Fein doesn't simply move from place to place, she is moved by every place she goes, and she has the artistic and literary skill to move the reader along with her. This is an excellent book by a very talented writer. And I read it without ever having to move at all.

Rabbi Rami Shapiro, author of Recovery, The Sacred Art

In *Life is a Trip*, Judith Fein provides a mouth-watering feast of journeys from Mexico to Micronesia, Vietnam to the splendors of Istanbul. Fein's writing is as honed as the sharpest knife edge. Many a writer would give their front teeth to match her eye for detail. She deserves great success with this book, not only because of its extraordinary sensitivity, but because it illuminates many lands in a new and remarkable way—from the inside out.

Tahir Shah, author of The Caliph's House, In Arabian Nights

Truth-seeking in travel appears to be Ms. Fein's mantra. The scenes she reveals in this fantastic volume are delightful, vulnerable, and at times, painful. She catches the tender details of human interactions and the pursuit of spirituality with grace for her subjects. Her writing inspires trust and those who want to be both heart and mind inspired will not be left wanting. A wonderful read!

Shannon Stowell, President, Adventure Travel Trade Association

I have learned over my 30-year career that the injured and the sick must do more to restore their health than take pills and submit to surgery. More frequently than most patients and physicians realize, the heart, soul and human spirit must be attended to in order for healing to be complete. Through Fein's travels, we see healing modalities from other parts of the world that pave the road for complete healing of the body and soul and are complementary to those that we are familiar with. *Life is a Trip* is a great read. I thoroughly enjoyed it!

Dana P. Launer, M.D., Scripps Memorial Hospital, La Jolla, California

From irreverence, reverence. That's the magic of Judith Fein's writing. Her unconventional view of the world and her grand sense of curiosity open doors to new adventures and understanding. She reminds us to look deeply into the differences that keep the world fascinating and the similarities that keep us unified. *Life Is a Trip* is a journey of the heart, soul and mind, and we are much the better for it.

Catharine M. Hamm, travel editor, "On the Spot," Los Angeles Times

For Judith Fein, every day on the road brings a new chance to touch and be touched by a magical world. These beautifully written travel stories and reflections work like 3-D glasses on a flat earth. More than a guide to transformative travel, this *is* transformative writing, as the author's keen capacity for amazement help us to see the world and our own lives as amazing.

Danny Rubin, writer of Groundhog Day

Although *Life if a Trip* is a short book, it is not necessarily a quick read. It is a deep and breathtaking invitation to a journey of appreciation. So take your time. Enter the world of transformational travel with Judith Fein as the most compassionate guide. You will travel with your ears, eyes, heart, and soul wide open. You will veer off the predictable track and venture beyond the course of a traditional guidebook. You will naturally become a part of the culture of the places you visit. The people you encounter, the habits you observe, the ways of life you absorb along the way, will change you profoundly. Yes, *Life is a Trip* is a wonderful read. It is a book of adventure, love, forgiveness, courage, friendship, respect, reflection, and challenge. More importantly, it is a guidebook to viewing (from a new perspective) your own life—the people in it and the choices you make. Through Judith's willingness to get "up close and personal" wherever she goes, she gives us the courage to step onto paths that truly do transform us ... not only while we are on the "trip" but also when we come home and re-consider the way we walk our own path.

Dale V. Atkins, Ph. D., NBC "Today Show" Psychologist

life is
a trip

the transformative
magic of travel

Judith Fein

Introduction

FOR MORE THAN TWELVE YEARS, I was a Hollywood screenwriter. By day, I spun tales of love, broken hearts, tragedy, triumph, and teen angst. I puttered around in a nightgown and brown fuzzy slippers that looked like bear claws. By night, I often went to screenings or swanky dinners, and my life was a swirl of pitching stories, drinking cocktails, taking meetings, negotiating contracts, and observing people so I could transform them into characters. Sounds glam, right? In fact, my experience was that it was a cutthroat, cruel, crazy biz designed to make a writer quake with insecurity and angst, and I felt as though my soul were being sucked out of me by an industrial vacuum cleaner.

One day, I woke up and knew I couldn't do it anymore. No more pitching, agents, lawyers, waiting, pain . . . or income. Nothing. I sat at home, my mind peering into the abyss, wondering if I had any talent or if I would ever work again. Months passed. The abyss grew deeper and blacker. I checked into a monastery in Arizona, took a vow of silence, and didn't speak for a week. And then, a strange call from my sister.

"Hey," she said. "There's a new national show on public radio about travel. You lived in Europe and Africa for ten years, you've always been a passionate traveler, and you have a long background in theatre. Why don't you record a story and send it in?"

"Why would they want me? The competition must be fierce. I have nothing to say," I moaned.

For lack of anything better to do, I wrote the tale of my recent silent retreat—where I managed to get into a food fight with a nun, was almost arrested on a dark, secluded road, and fantasized about why the statue of St. Francis frowned. My husband, Paul, and I performed voice-overs, so we had a small recording studio in our home. I performed my monastic adventures in front of a mike and sent the tape to the show, *The Savvy Traveler*.

Four days later the phone rang. They really liked the piece, wanted to use it, asked me to be a regular contributor to the show, and gave me my first assignment. The pay was very low, the prestige high, and I loved it.

For several years, I traveled every chance I got and I tumbled into wild and wacky situations, which I recorded and then transformed into radio pieces. I earned about as much as a teenager who waters his vacationing neighbors' plants. Then an idea struck me: what if I parlayed the prestige into pitching travel stories to newspapers and magazines?

It worked, sort of. I sold a few articles to newspapers, and one or two of them asked me if I had any other articles. And the fact that I had a few outlets for my travel stories inspired me to do more traveling. I didn't even know that what I was doing had a name—"travel journalist"—and that it was a bona fide way to make a living.

Since that time, I have written for more than eighty-five publications worldwide and garnered awards for my articles. I write about food, culture, art, history, spirituality, luxury, off-the-beaten path travel, exotic destinations, people, celebrations, special events, and anything else I am lucky enough to discover. Paul and I have made travel films, given many talks, and he sells photographs from our trips. Sometimes we work fifteen-hour days. I basically have two states of being: on the road or on the computer.

One day, an editor said to me, "Your articles are different from other travel journalists' because you really know how to tell a story."

I grinned, and I thanked my years in Hollywood for teaching me how to do that—how to tell a story about a place and the people who live there.

"You know how to travel deeply," said another editor.

I had never really thought about it. My interest in travel had always been a fascination for what lies beneath the surface. I relished spontaneous meetings, arrows pointing me in a different direction from the one I had planned. Even mishaps. In South Africa, Paul got an ear infection and he couldn't fly for a month. Panic. Stranded in South Africa. Opportunity. Adventure. We went to a Zulu *sangoma* (healer), stumbled upon an Ndebele village where the women are artists and paint geometric designs on their houses, visited townships, met locals everywhere.

In Switzerland, some unexpected bad weather got in the way of touring, but led us to inquire about how locals predicted the weather. The next thing we knew, we were in the home of a *wetterschmecker* (literally a "weather taster") and entered a world of people who predicted the weather based upon signs in nature—like the wool on a sheep or the way branches hang from a tree. Locally, they are also known as the "weather frogs."

In Tunisia, we missed a desert festival, but I had a chance meeting with a Bedouin horseman, which gave me precious entry into a beautiful and ancient culture, which led to a correspondence with the horseman that went on for years. In the Israeli desert, I was disappointed because we arrived too late to catch photos of the sunset, but I ended up in a tent with a sheikh, exchanging ideas about marriage over several bracing cups of tea and a meal of chicken couscous cooked on an open fire.

In Ireland, a comment by a guide about the truth of the nineteenth-century potato famine led me on a focused and fascinating trip through the country, where I discovered how the Irish people were starved to death and why they really came to America. In New Zealand, a keen interest in the Maori people and an exploration of their origination stories led to the joy of us getting "adopted" into an extended Maori family, who remain close to our hearts and lives today.

Eventually, all of these experiences resulted in published articles. And that encouraged me to be continually on the lookout for stories, to find the characters, history, tales, and teachings that lurk and shimmer and are waiting to be discovered underneath the surface of our travels. Of course, I always hoped that the stories I wrote would enrich the lives of readers, but I knew for sure that they enhanced my life and kept me in a perpetual state of wide-eyed excitement. I was a hopeless, incurably-addicted traveler.

The difference between being a tourist and a traveler is that a traveler is open to unplanned experience and doesn't have her nose stuck in a guidebook, tracking down famous sites. She ventures out from behind glass windows (in hotels and touring buses) and meets people. She connects. The difference between a traveler and a travel journalist is that the latter is always searching for stories. But it occurred to me that *any* traveler can travel like a journalist—looking for cues and clues, diving into new cultures, and coming home with great stories and new ways of responding to life.

Maybe the marks of a good traveler—whether one treks for pleasure or as a profession—are the stories he experiences and retells and what he learns from those stories.

"How do you become a travel writer?" people always ask me. I decided that I would like to answer that question in order to let others know how to do it. I want to focus on the *way* of the travel writer, rather than the note-taking, interviewing, information-gathering process. I hope to encourage others to step out of their comfort zones and really experience the places they are visiting and the people who live there.

I understand that not everyone wants to be a travel writer, but the skills that a travel journalist has can help anyone to travel more richly, in a safe, satisfying, and spontaneous way. And the traveler is sure to come home with fascinating stories and experiences that can transform his life and touch the lives of those around him.

In this book, I'm sharing with you what I absorbed and brought back from key experiences and encounters during my years of travel—experiences that have shaped me, opened me up to the world and been put to the test many times. I hope these experiences will touch you and help you as you navigate the challenges of travel and traveling through life. Maybe the experiences will inspire you . . . whether you are on the road or never venture beyond your hometown.

I live to leave . . . and I invite you to join me on my adventures.

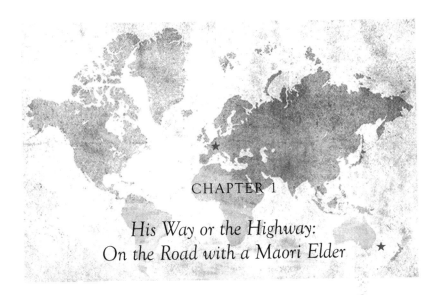

CHAPTER 1

His Way or the Highway: On the Road with a Maori Elder

CHRISTINE WILSON HAD A VISION—a travel vision whose participants included a gaggle of fidgety, vomiting infants; handfuls of potentially incompatible adults; a few guardians who were strong enough to manage the unpredictable rages that sometimes erupted from a deeply traumatized brain; and Christine's husband, John Wilson, an unflappable Maori elder.

This odd parade of pilgrims waddled, crawled, bounded, and walked into three aging, rented camper vans that had the annoying habit of breaking down. The children spewed and pooed, the women frowned, the men stared intently into the campers' frequently failing engines, fiddling with this and that wire. And, throughout it all, Christine Wilson exuded confidence that all would be well, and elder John smiled and flicked his woolen cap. Sure enough, the vans eventually hit the road again until the next automotive collapse.

Christine's travel vision was broad, chaotic, and inspired by history. In the mid-nineteenth century, British immigrants and convicts began arriving in New Zealand. The former were seeking a better life and they were accepted as long-term residents and citizens. The latter—young offenders—were roundly rejected and it was difficult for them to find work. Most of them were guilty of petty crimes and they had been raised with poverty and deprivation.

As more European immigrants arrived, there was a degree of hanky-panky, love, lust, and marriage between them, their descendants, and the Maori tribes who had populated New Zealand for many centuries. The Maori were a robust Polynesian culture, and their tattoos, taboos, wood carvings of ancestors, pride and proficiency at seafaring, navigation, oration, hospitality, as well as their custom of dining on human flesh made them seem quite exotic compared to the more reserved Europeans (called *Pakeha* by the Maori). There are few records documenting the mixing and matching of Pakeha and Maori, but Pakeha today will often tell you about Maori ancestors in their family trees and Maori will acknowledge their Pakeha forebears.

As is most often the case with indigenous cultures, the Maori were tricked and abused by the colonial powers (in this case, the British Crown). More bellicose and efficient than most, they have refused to take broken treaties lying down. Their fight to regain land, money, language, and dignity goes on today. But, at the same time, they are intertwined with Pakeha culture, and many Maori have Pakeha spouses.

Perhaps because she is a Brit who married a Maori man, Christine Wilson became very interested in the historic blending of Pakeha and Maori—two cultures she admired greatly.

"I thought that my husband and his kin might be interested in going back to Europe to find out about their Pakeha roots," she said simply.

Other Kiwis (New Zealanders) have certainly thought about a roots route before, but Christine moved from musing to action. She booked flights, rented camper vans, and peopled them with an assortment of folks connected by blood, affinity or, in a few cases, smoldering antipathy.

John Wilson's son, Carin, and daughter, Virginia (from his first Pakeha wife), were among the chosen. Carin's wife, Jenney, and Virginia's daughter came along as well. Accompanying them through ancestral lands were Christine's children from her first marriage to a Polynesian—Natasha (with her three young boys), Hans (who was navigating a born-again Christian phase), and Antony (a young man of indomitable spirit who had been run over by a transport truck when he was a child and suffered horrific brain damage). There was also Kristina (the semi-estranged wife of Christine's son Nicholas) and her three daughters.

In addition, Christine invited her friend Maria, a singer with Lebanese roots; Maori marrieds Russell and Becky (who were going to help Antony on the trip and also share the driving); Kip, a Maori guitar player and singer; Marta and Brandon (she, an adept of diverse spiritual practices and he, a Canadian man with First Nations ancestry who played his drum a lot); my husband Paul, and me.

"I carefully chose the pilgrims who would come with us," Christine explained. "This isn't a trip, you understand. It's a pilgrimage."

Paul and I had never met Christine or anyone else before the pilgrimage. Christine had read my published writings, began a correspondence with me, and sent us tickets to fly to Frankfurt and meet the questers in her vision.

Paul and I had never traveled in a camper van, but we should have known that clumps of people could not sleep comfortably—if they could sleep at all—in those tight, flimsy, traveling boxes.

We met Christine and the clan at the airport in Frankfurt. John, tanned, manly, vigorous, and gentlemanly at almost eighty years old, greeted us with a *haka*—a Maori war whoop. He ritually slapped his chest and thighs and rolled out his considerable tongue. Originally designed to intimidate the enemies of the warlike Maori, the haka delighted Paul and me. And a small crowd of people, who probably thought that the water in the airport was spiked and they were hallucinating, gathered to watch the shouting, breast-beating, panting, and eye-rolling.

Then, as his beaming, blonde wife stood proudly next to him, John presented Paul and me with beautiful pendants made of large, polished *pounamu* (jade). In Maori culture, as I understand it, a piece of pounamu is considered to be a *taonga* (treasure), which has *mana* and also bestows mana on its owner. Defining or translating mana is a tricky business. It was explained to me as a combination of personal prestige and character.

If you are so inclined, you can purchase a piece of pounamu from a shop in New Zealand, but its mana comes to you when you receive it as a gift. The pounamu is found in a river on the south island of New Zealand, and only the Maori are licensed to gather it.

Being presented with two pieces of pounamu by an elder of the Ngati Awa was no small honor for us. For many years afterwards, our pounamu pendants bobbed along on our chests wherever we went—including into the shower. Christine said that the pounamu would change color after contact with the flesh, which it did. It became burnished by the heat and oils of our bodies.

But back to the roots trip. We flew from Germany to Italy to meet up with our vans and, when it was time to sleep, the van drivers pulled into the parking lot of a fast food restaurant. There, under the glaring lights, Christine's crew bedded down for the night. Used to sleeping in close quarters on the floors of *wharenui* (meeting houses on *marae*, sacred Maori ceremonial and gathering spaces), a chunk of our traveling companions fell asleep. The others, by turn, and according to their ages, drummed, threw up, cried, cackled, shat, and yakked.

Paul and I wandered from one van to the next, desperately trying to find a quiet corner where we could stretch out. There was no such place. Limbs flew in our faces, body parts were illuminated by parking lot flood lights, and we spent a sleepless night, after an equally sleepless night flight from the United States to Germany.

I was panicked from lack of privacy, and after thirteen years of marriage, Paul and I didn't need long discourses: "No way," he said. "I'm outta here," I concurred.

When Christine has a vision, she doesn't permit it to become polluted by the inability of two foreign wimps to handle group sleep. "From now on," she announced, "our two American guests will sleep in hotels."

She was true to her word. Thereafter, our travel days ended in hotel rooms where, blessing the generosity of Christine and acknowledging our guilt about our travel mates who did not have the luxury of accommodations, we genuflected before the Deus ex Mattress and collapsed.

The potential conflict with us was averted, but a soup of roiling emotions was simmering in the camper vans. Two words tell the tale: blended families. I always thought that "blending" entailed the combining of elements to make a smooth new entity. It turns out that, in some cases, blending means that the parts vigorously separate (by means of seething) to form a new, disunified whole.

And this was the case in those three camper vans, for which Christine had paid an exorbitant amount of money to give wheels to her vision.

The unexpressed hostilities that ricocheted through our dis-united family of pilgrims were immediately recognizable to me from my own family, which, although not blended, harbored enough anger to encompass four or five families at least.

The chaos of Christine's children seemed to unnerve the more reserved offspring of John's former union. Lists of past hurts and oversights were branded on the hearts of some of the various children, and the daily proximity of the wounded who were thrown together by John and Christine loving each other became untenable. Natasha's son fell and gashed his head open; Antony had a flip-out and socked Christine; Maria's feelings were hurt and she had a little crying jag; Russell refused to drive another inch until he had more "evidence" than a general direction in which to drive; Marta was communing with Spirit; Brandon was drumming, Christine was darting left and right as she tried to keep the troops in line.

Those of you who at one time or another belonged to a family unit can certainly envision a domestic volcano about to blow. Now imagine that volcano about to erupt in three flimsy, moving boxes.

John Wilson seemed to be oblivious to the tensions in the campers. He sat with his hands folded, occasionally nodding off, his woolen cap balanced perfectly on his head. He'd served as a fighter pilot in the Royal Air Force, was a lawyer negotiating with the Crown for Ngati Awa claims, had been divorced, dealt with children, and had a penchant for fast cars and fast driving. Having seen and done it all, nothing rattled this elder.

It was on the *autostrada* in Italy, I think, that John suddenly turned to his wife and proclaimed, "Chrissy, we have to stop the vans."

There was no place to stop on the freeway except the precarious slice of green island that separates traffic racing in one direction from cars careening in the other. The vans swerved and turned and bumped up on the tiny island as John calmly alit from the lead van.

I braced for what I knew was coming: a family screaming match where each person aired every offense visited upon him since his exodus from the womb. I wondered if I could slip out of my body and watch it all from a passing cloud or dive down under the freeway asphalt and wait it out. Even though I have had spasms of anger myself when someone poked at one of my buttons, I dread angry outbursts. Some think they are cathartic, but I consider them to be approximately as appealing as botulism.

John Wilson motioned for everyone to sit on the grass in a circle.

Obeying the elder, the fuming, hurt, baffled, tired, teary pilgrims sat en masse—and, truth be told, since the island was longer than it was wide, it was an oblong circle.

Ten, nine, eight, seven, six, five, four . . . and before I hit three in my crisis countdown, the elder spoke. He wasn't yelling, despite the din of the BMWs and Fiats roaring by. He wasn't—as he sometimes did—pounding his cane and waxing eloquent in Maori oratorical style. Incredibly, John Wilson was singing.

There was a beat of silence and then Christine joined in, followed by the lilting voices of Maria and Kip. Carin began to sing and his sister Virginia chimed in, and then Jenney did as well. Antony began to bellow gleefully, and Natasha and the boys burst into song with Russell and Becky holding up their corner of the chorus. Not only didn't I know the words to the Maori song or the melody, but even if I had, I would have been too stunned to sing as the clan in the campers began to literally harmonize.

One song followed the next and pretty soon the family panic had turned into a picnic. Faces that were tense moments before relaxed, arms were slung around shoulders, and I was sitting in the middle of a (freeway) isle of *bonhommerie*.

Elder John Wilson was a native trickster, a wily psychologist who had sung swords into smiles. By the time the singing waned and the talking began, tempers were defused, hurts were temporarily forgotten, and we all boarded the vans until the next physical or emotional breakdown.

John Wilson died a year ago, just shy of his ninetieth birthday. Christine claims that they are—if possible—even closer in death than they were in life.

"He is in me, with me all the time," she says. "We are one."

I will never forget John performing a haka—with his jawbone protruding, his big eyes bulging out, and his breath rolling out over his long tongue. But, most of all, I will remember the way he avoided conflict by singing. I, who am among the most direct of people, understood from the Maori elder that sometimes a circuitous route can be more effective: song or play or joking or storytelling can soften a tough situation and make it manageable.

Shortly after I came home from the roots trip, I was, metaphorically speaking, back in the camper vans again. A couple I know was on the verge of either breakup or murder; it was hard to tell which. They sat in my living room, glowering at each other, and then unleashed a torrent of accusations replete with finger-pointing, rising voices, and faces twisted into grimaces of anger and resentment. After they had exploded at each other, they turned to me, each trying to solicit an outsider's support for his or her point of view.

I sat quietly for a moment, and then, instead of addressing the marital discord, I thought of John Wilson and suggested we all go for a walk. They hesitated for a moment . . . and then agreed.

We put on our jackets and went outdoors. I led them to a park that is cattycorner to our house, and, as we walked around the periphery, we saw a couple with two dogs and two toddlers. The couple spoke to the dogs and toddlers with the same words and same intonations, and the canines and kids lined up behind them in a neat row. I burst out laughing. My friends burst out laughing. They exchanged a quick glance. The man remarked that one of the dogs reminded him of their pooch. The woman agreed. They began to talk about their beloved four-legged. And, as they did so, the hostility melted. Just like that.

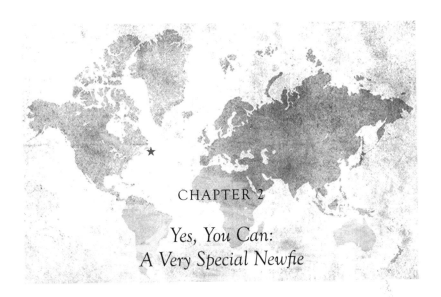

CHAPTER 2

Yes, You Can:
A Very Special Newfie

A S FAR AS I COULD TELL, the only thing Ed English was missing was half a finger. He had lost it when he was sawing. His wife retrieved the severed digit and off they went to the hospital . . . with Ed at the wheel. The doctors convinced him that he'd be better off without the mass of nerves, muscles, and tendons that made up his finger, so he shrugged and agreed with them.

I'm not sure what the docs did with the piece of finger, but Ed said kids love to see him place his knuckle stump under his nostril; it gives the illusion that the rest of his finger is crawling up inside his nose. Sooner or later, the kids figure out that there is no crawling, no finger, and Ed is an adult dude with a wicked sense of kid humor.

Ed lives in the Gros Morne National Park area of Newfoundland and he's the local Donald Trump with much better hair. He was once in a bookstore when his wife called on his cell phone to say she'd found a cool house. "Buy it," he urged her, and she did. He also bought a lighthouse and half an island, sight unseen.

Quirpon Island, which I like to call "Ed's island," is off the northern tip of Newfoundland. In late June to early July, it's blessed with icebergs, whales, and Ed's kayaks, which you can reserve at Ed's lighthouse or, more correctly, Ed's lighthouse keeper's house, which he has turned into an inn.

To get there, you catch a boat at St. Antony's. Depending upon the weather and the size of the boat that shows up, you head for a dock near the lighthouse or a dock several foot hours away. The day I went, the small wooden boat stopped at the far side of Quirpon, which, by the way, rhymes with "harpoon."

I felt a couple of levels of dismay as Ed helped me out of the boat. First, I had ignorantly packed for summer and it was the kind of weather you expect when you are drinking eggnog and decorating a tree. I was wearing wafer-thin pants, a quick-drying shirt, and Crocs. The ugly, Swiss-cheese-holed Crocs I had sworn never to wear, ended up being the shoes I never took off, and I had worn them so insistently that they had no tread left. Second, Ed informed me, it could take anywhere from thirty-five minutes to four hours to hike to the lighthouse.

"I don't think I can do it," I whined, and Ed sort of made a clicking noise with his tongue and mumbled, "We'll work it out."

"It's muddy," I protested. "I'm carrying a five-pound handbag, a book, and . . ."

"No problem," Ed said. He grabbed my bag, book, and he would have grabbed me and put me in his backpack if I had been capable of folding up that compactly.

The Crocs and the cold weren't my only problems. Give me flat terrain and I can walk until the Messiah comes. But add a steep incline, and some exercise-activated asthma gnomes slow me to a crawl. There were hills on Quirpon. It was a "bear climbed over the mountain" sort of island; you climbed up one hill and there was another. And on and on. If you were Ed, a mountain goat, you could get off the boat at 5:30, run over the hills, and arrive at the lighthouse in thirty-five minutes, just in time for supper. If you were I, you probably wouldn't arrive until dessert or brandy.

Did I forget to mention black biting things? I'd killed off dozens before I'd made it up the first hill and they lay ugly and dead, where they met their untimely end—on my neck, scalp, and forehead. I had forgotten to pack bug spray. I didn't think no-see-ums or mosquitoes, or whatever they were, flew that far north.

I was cold, bitten, panting, and trying not to slide in my treadless Crocs. Ed was whistling and cheerfully telling local tales of murders and suicides, people stranded and having their limbs lopped off to avoid gangrene. I tried to douse my imagination, which was on fire.

If my grandmother had been the type who baked sponge cake, this is how it would have felt underfoot if I had walked on it. The terrain on Quirpon Island wasn't exactly bog. More like springy lichen. It was quite unlike any other surface I'd ever experienced, except briefly in the Canadian Arctic, when I was so cold I wore seven layers of clothes and I couldn't appreciate the subtlety beneath my four pairs of socks and hiking boots. My Crocs sank in, my Crocs came out. Up. Down. Up. Down. If it had been flat, I would have bounced my way to the lighthouse. But since it was impossible to bounce uphill, I proceeded like a Slinky for the first hour.

"How much longer?" I asked Ed, feeling like a six-year-old in the back of a car that daddy was driving.

"Well, it could be some more hours," Ed replied. Ignoring my barely suppressed panic, he bent over, plucked some golden berries and proffered them to me. "These are bake apples," he said. "Also called cloudberries."

"I don't suppose they're covered in moose shit or anything?" I asked.

"Nope. No moose on Quirpon Island."

"Elk?"

"Not a chance. You might encounter some birds or mink, but cross my heart, no mink shit either."

I ate one bake apple, then two. They were soft and sweet, melting evenly on the palate.

Next came blueberries, then partridgeberries. And, as I savored them, Ed pointed out large purple fireweeds, purple-stemmed aster, bluebells, black crowberries, and bunchberries (also called crackerberries), which made up the Quirpon ground cover.

Every time Ed introduced me to a different weed or flower, I had an excuse to pause and shore up my breath for the next hill. Two and a half hours after disembarking from the boat, we arrived at the lighthouse. I was secretly proud of myself for braving the cold, crumbling Crocs, mud, wind, and hills. As the three graces who run the lighthouse keeper's house served a traditional Jigg's Dinner (made of beef, potato, turnip, peas porridge, and cabbage), I settled in and decided I was going to like Ed's island.

Until the next day. A cold wind that blew no one any good came howling in, the sky was Porta-Potty gray, and it began to rain. I selected a book from Ed's library and dug in. Ed, who is a voracious reader, suggested I might want to have a look at the picture-book-pretty-white-trimmed-with-red lighthouse and the area around it.

The next thing I knew, I had borrowed a jacket and moose hide gloves and was hiking. I scampered over some rocks and kept climbing higher and higher until I could see out over the ocean where whales swam and icebergs often spend a few weeks or a month. It began to rain. My aging Crocs were slipping and sliding. Suddenly Ed appeared, leaping over the rocks, wearing nothing more than shorts and a T-shirt. Without saying anything, he held out an arm. I grabbed it so hard I almost separated it from its socket. And, just like that, oblivious to the rain, wind, cold, and mud, Ed helped me over the rain-lashed rocks, whistling merrily as I inched along.

I kept thinking that Ed must have moods. No one can be that relentlessly cheery and helpful. If you want a book, some information, a special drink, or food, Ed provides it. Effortlessly. I leaned forward to see if there were gnash marks on his teeth or if his brow was furrowed. Nothing.

"Want to climb up the lighthouse?" Ed asked.

Hmm. I did want to go to the top, but it was that damn climbing thing again. And cold. And dark. I wondered if I could do it.

"Just don't fall in the hole," Ed laughed as he unlocked the lighthouse door and ushered me inside. Then he disappeared.

When I got to the top, I gazed through the window of the lighthouse and saw Ed. He was running over his island, maybe going to fetch something or perhaps for exercise or the sheer joy of the run.

The last day I was in Newfoundland, I mentioned to Ed that I was interested in learning more about Sir Wilfred Grenfell, a swashbuckling doctor/preacher/artist/writer/humanitarian who, in 1892, had brought medical care and social services to the folks who had neither in Labrador and Newfoundland. He empowered women to start a cottage industry with their skills of hooking rugs and producing crafts. He yanked fishermen from the clutches of merchants who kept them dependent and impoverished, and he taught the fishermen to form their own cooperatives. He braved ice and storms, traveled by dogsled, slept in snow, and risked his life to help impecunious fishermen and natives. Once, stranded on ice with his dogsled, he had to kill his beloved dogs and use their fur to survive the frigid weather. With their bones, he built a flagpole to signal his distress. Later, he erected a monument to them.

Shortly after I mentioned Sir Grenfell, Ed pressed a book about the doctor into my hands.

"I'm afraid I can't get it back to you before I leave," I told him.

"No worry," he assured me. "You can read it during the water taxi crossing."

Later that afternoon, I took a water taxi from Woody Point to Norris Point in scenic Gros Morne National Park. Although I loved looking at the little shoreline towns with their colorful clotheslines and white churches trimmed in black, I opened the book and damn if I didn't finish it by the time the water taxi reached the shore. I'd been speed-reading for less than twenty minutes, and, as Ed had predicted, I'd completed the thin volume.

I was at the Lobster Cove Head lighthouse in Norris Point, waiting for Ed to pick me up after I'd attended a rug-hooking workshop, when I mentioned to a park ranger that I knew Ed and he was the most gonzo guy I had encountered in eons.

"The secret about Ed," the ranger said, "is that he makes you believe you can do anything."

That was it. She had articulated what it was about Ed that made me hike, climb, brave the elements, and read at lightning speed. He treated me as though there were no doubt I could do anything. No fuss. No discussion. He smiled, whistled, held out a hand. It was obvious I was going to do the things Ed suggested, and I did them.

A few months later, I was with a friend who had recently published a book and she was invited to speak about it and her life at a conference. She couldn't sleep or eat; she'd worked herself into a frenzy of fear, inadequacy, and public performance panic.

"I know I'll screw up," she kept saying. "Even if I write it all out—and I hate it when other speakers do that—I'll lose my place. I'll look ridiculous. No one will want to buy my book."

I smiled inwardly as I thought of Ed.

"When you told me about how you wrote plays as a kid and performed them for yourself in front of a mirror, I thought it was touching and charming," I said.

"You did?"

"Of course. I especially loved the details about how you raided your mother's and sister's closets and dressed up for the show."

"I almost strangled myself wrapping my sister's boas around my neck. And I stuffed a pair of socks in my mother's shoes because they were so big. Do you think I could start my talk with that?"

I grinned. She was off and running. And we never had to discuss whether she could or couldn't do it. I had pulled an Ed English. Thank you, Ed.

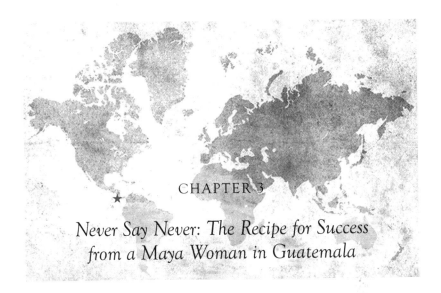

CHAPTER 3

Never Say Never: The Recipe for Success from a Maya Woman in Guatemala

THE FIRST TIME I WENT TO SAN ANTONIO DE AGUAS CALIENTES in the Highlands of Guatemala, my heart ripped open as though it had been held shut by Velcro all my life.

I had hopped on a "chicken bus" in Antigua, Guatemala. If heaven were in Central America, the angels would hang out in Antigua. Nestled in the lap of Agua (water) and Fuego (fire) volcanoes, paved with cobblestones, dotted with churches that look like ornate and sugary wedding cakes, home to language schools, a posh hotel in a converted monastery, restaurants, and shop opps for the most meager to the most lavish budgets, Antigua is the languid dream of every traveler who wants to bathe in beauty while surrounded by bubbles of exotic and fascinating culture.

At the edge of town is a depot where gaily-painted old school buses wait for the onslaught of locals who drag groceries, vegetables, and live chickens on board to transport them to their villages.

I randomly selected a bus and found, to my delight, that it was packed with Maya people who were going home after a day of work, selling, trading, bartering, or shopping in Antigua.

A trained eye can tell which village a Maya person comes from by the clothing he wears. The women wear brilliantly colored, intricately woven and designed *huipiles* or sleeveless tops. According to a woman who sat on the bus with two chickens in a bag on her lap, the ones I found most appealing came from San Antonio de Aguas Calientes. Furthermore, she informed me, our bus was stopping there, and she'd be happy to tell me when we arrived.

We chatted for about half an hour as Maya people got on and off the bus. I loved the way they looked—small, with large eyes, mocha skin, thick, black hair and open faces. They had been through the horrors of colonialism, war, massacres, and violence of every stripe, yet they still were friendly and approachable.

I got off the chicken bus next to a seventeenth-century baroque church and saw a sign pointing to a shop that sold textiles. The door was closed and, when I knocked, it was opened by a diminutive woman. For me to call another person "diminutive" is no ordinary occurrence. When I stand up straight, I am five feet tall, so I would estimate that the woman was about four feet eight, give or take a few inches.

She greeted me in her native Cakchiquel and explained to me in Spanish (I understood a few word clusters here and there) that I was standing in a women's textile cooperative. Most or all of the women were widowed and they survived by weaving the placemats, tablecloths, handbags, men's and women's clothes, belts, and huipiles I saw on the walls and display tables around me.

The woman, whose name was María Elena Godinez Lopez, showed me how the backstrap looms worked. She sat on the floor, a thick belt around her waist tied to a vertical wooden beam, her dexterous fingers weaving on the loom in front of her. The huipile, which she had been working on for several months, was woven on two sides and was adorned with dazzling fruits, trees, parrots, and flowers. When I asked how long the backstrap loom had been used by Maya people, she chopped through the air from left to right, indicating many, many generations.

María Elena showed me her kitchen (the textile showroom was part of her house); it was a small area with a dirt floor. Three stones on the floor formed the base of an open fire where she made corn tortillas for her family. She demonstrated her tortilla-making technique, and the little kitchen filled with an agreeable slapping sound as she transferred the corn dough from one hand to the other, shaping it into flat discs. Then she rapidly cooked them over the fire and handed me one to taste. She grinned broadly when I ran my tongue over my lips and made a "yum, yum" sound.

Before I left, María Elena said, "Tomorrow there will be a procession for Assumption Day. Why don't you come back?" As soon as I exited her house cum workshop, a Maya family emerged from the baroque church, carefully laying down brightly colored flower petals and pine needles to form a carpet. They explained the carpet was for the procession for Assumption Day. I knew I had to return.

Late the next afternoon, I took a chicken bus back to San Antonio and alit near the church. I knocked on María Elena's door, and she came out attired in a magnificent huipil. The procession had started inside the heart of the village at someone's house, she said, and it hadn't yet arrived at the church.

I walked with her down the town's main artery and through side streets until I heard the rumble of drums, the blaring of trumpets, and the lilting sound of flutes. Then St. Anthony, the patron saint of the town, appeared in a thick cloud of incense smoke. Twelve Maya men, six on each side, were carrying a statue of the saint on a long litter, their shoulders wedged into scalloped openings in the wooden platform.

Behind them was another litter carried by eighteen Maya women. They were transporting the Virgin Mary; the festival commemorates the day God took her body and soul to heaven.

I couldn't take my eyes off the Maya women. Convivial, resplendent in their woven clothing, they were concentrating on the important task of carrying and honoring their universal Mother. In San Antonio, as elsewhere in Guatemala, the Maya practice a syncretized form of Catholicism. It blends their ancestral religion with the faith brought to the country during the Spanish conquest in the sixteenth century.

I found the procession riveting. The smoke created a mysterious, holy aura around the saints, and the tiny women who carried the incense were elegantly adorned with folded-up textiles on their heads. I followed the parade from the sidelines and was walking alongside Mary when María Elena turned to me and asked, "Would you like to carry the Virgin?"

I blinked. I nodded. María Elena tapped one of the porters on the sleeve, and she slipped out of the shoulder notch and gestured for me to take her place. I looked at María Elena uncertainly.

"Yes, yes, go, go," she reassured me.

I slid into the empty space, joining the Maya women, feeling as though I had a serious job to do—helping in some minuscule way to perpetuate the traditions in San Antonio. It was then that the aforementioned Velcro opening of my heart took place. I was so moved and touched that I had been allowed to share a moment of the enduring Maya culture.

I carried the saint for about twenty minutes, and then my shoulder began to hurt. I was much taller than the other women, so I had to carry the brunt of the weight of the wooden litter. María Elena took my place, and I returned to the sidelines.

When the procession was over, I stopped at María Elena's house to say "thank you." We hugged and I was surprised when she stopped me at the door. "May I ask you an important question?" she inquired.

"Of course."

"Tell me how I can see the world the way you do."

I was a bit nonplussed. How could I explain to a woman who barely eked out a living by weaving textiles, who had no computer and little or no education, how to become a travel journalist?

"You want me to tell you about schools for journalism?" I asked her. "I'm not sure about the possibilities in your country, but I can try to find out."

María Elena shook her head. "I don't know about journalism. I just want to see the world. How do I do it?"

I explained to her about passports and visas and that it often takes a long time to obtain them and it can be costly.

"How do I get to your country to visit you?" María Elena asked.

I often dread that question when I am traveling. I live in an apartment without a guest bedroom. I am on the road a lot and frequently leave without much advance notice, so it's difficult to make plans. I certainly have hosted people I've met in my travels, but I work on deadlines and if a visitor arrives who knows no English, has no transportation or money, I have to be selective about offering to be a full-time host and tour guide. So I didn't know quite what to say to María Elena. I gave her my business card and said I would tell everyone I met in Guatemala to visit her village and buy her textiles so she could save money to see the world.

I actually returned shortly with a group of fifteen people, all of whom bought clothes, bags, and placemats from María Elena, but she was stand-offish and hardly seemed to know who I was. I thanked her again for her kindness to me and left.

When I got back to the U.S.A., the phone calls began. Once or several times a week, María Elena phoned to ask if she could visit. I had a hard time understanding Spanish in person, but on the phone it was next to impossible. I frantically thumbed through a dictionary as we spoke, not wanting her to spend money while I fumbled to communicate. I told her that Paul and I would be traveling a lot over the next year and I couldn't make plans. I kept repeating "visa" and "passport," hoping she would understand that she couldn't travel without them.

The more María Elena called, the sadder I felt. She was frittering away her hard-earned quetzals on a pipe dream. How could she ever see the world, except in her imagination?

One night, months later, María Elena called and asked me if I would write a letter inviting her to the U.S. "Of course," I said, wondering how I had become part of her travel fantasy. "I will mail you a letter next week."

"No, no, no," she insisted. "I want so badly to travel. I will find someone who has email and you can send the letter to that person for me."

Several days later, an email arrived. María Elena had indeed found someone to send an email on her behalf, which reiterated her request for a letter of invitation. I did what I had promised to do and wrote the note. Then I left the country and, for much of the year, was on the road.

Months later, when I was home for a stay, the phone rang and it was María Elena. I'd rehearsed in my mind what I would say: "María Elena, I am exhausted. We've been traveling very far and I need to settle in, answer my emails, pay my bills, file stories. Please forgive me if I can't invite you at this time."

But María Elena didn't give me time to deliver my prepared speech. "I called to say 'thank you,'" she said. "Thanks to your encouragement and your invitation I was able to visit California. It was wonderful to travel and to see your country."

She spoke so fast that I didn't understand how she got her passport, visa, and airline ticket to the U.S. With whom did she stay? Was it a relative? A new friend? An old friend?

Frankly, I was in awe of María Elena. Against all odds, she pursued her dream relentlessly. It was, after all, *her* dream and no one—least of all me—had the power to discourage her. I wouldn't be surprised if I were in Paris one day, craning my neck as I looked up at the Eiffel Tower and there, on top, I saw María Elena waving down at me.

After my last phone call with María Elena, I began to think of other people who were raised without the benefits of education and exposure, who had pursued what seemed to be impossible dreams.

There was a young girl I met in Tunisia, in a remote area near the border of Algeria, when an "Internet bus," outfitted with computers and connections, came riding through her town. It was the first time many of the kids had laid hands on a computer, and of course they were excited and mesmerized.

The girl lived a subsistence existence with her widowed mother and brothers, and the mother confided that she had sacrificed everything to give her children an education. She had no idea what the Internet was or what a computer looked like, but she was thrilled when her daughter climbed into the classroom-on-wheels for an educational experience.

I interviewed the girl when she exited from the bus. "How did you like it?" I asked, expecting a one or two-word answer.

"I will learn this!" she said. "I want to be rich, I want to be famous, I want to be a star. I'll go to a great school, I'll study something important, and I'll make my mother proud of me."

I smiled indulgently, not really believing that any of it could happen. But, to my amazement, it did. She went to school in the capital city of

Tunis, got a nursing degree, and began practicing in a clinic. A few weeks ago I got an invitation to be her friend on Facebook.

I have taken a vow: Never will I ever underestimate the power of anyone's dreams. Not even my own.

CHAPTER 4

The Last Judgment on Mog Mog in Micronesia

OVER THE PAST FEW DECADES, I have been privileged to witness two births, a handful of baby-welcoming ceremonies, many marriages, and I have accompanied more than one person to the final threshold of life. All the trivia of quotidian existence dissolved as I participated in the embracing holiness of these events. So now, whenever I travel, I always inquire about family celebrations, religious pageants or observances and pivotal ceremonies because it seems to me that this is where real life happens. When I am fortunate enough to be invited to participate, I find myself interacting with people in a context that is meaningful and authentic. I am no longer a tourist. I am forced to be real, present, aware and observant. And I am always deeply grateful for the opportunity.

A few years ago when I was on the island of Yap, in Micronesia—9,394 miles from New York and 6,883 from Los Angeles—I made a request of the locals with whom I spent time: "Do you know of anyone who just had a baby, is getting married, or has died and wouldn't mind if I attended their ceremony?"

They shook their heads. Undaunted, I asked every person I met, but the answer was always the same.

"How about the outer islands? Any life ceremonies there?" I asked.

I was informed that the outer islands were remote and largely inaccessible. Every few months, a boat named the Micronesia Spirit came to Yap to transport folks to the islands, but there was no fixed schedule. If you happened to hear about a crossing, you could book passage. Otherwise, no way. A few expats who lived on the island of Yap said they had never been able to visit the outer islands, even though they had tried.

Just as I was about to give up any hope of witnessing a life ceremony, the manager of the hotel where I was staying knocked on my door. "There is a funeral ship going to the outer island of Mog Mog," she declared, beaming, "and you are booked on it. Congratulations!"

When I told some locals of my good fortune, they turned ashen. "Hasn't anyone warned you about the Micronesia Spirit?" they asked. I shook my head and laughed.

Two days later, at dusk, I was on my way. I watched as a coffin was solemnly carried onto the three-tiered boat and then I boarded the Micronesia Spirit with a rolled-up yoga mat, a sandwich, and two bottles of water. The ship, licensed to transport 150 mortals, was dangerously over-crowded with close to 250 passengers. It seemed that everyone but me had staked out a place to sleep, and most were already lying on overlapping woven mats or flattened cardboard boxes so that the decks were a human carpet. I'd been told that you never step over a prostrate Micronesian, so how could I walk around the ship without stepping over bodies? I stood still and plotted what I would do to get through the next fourteen hours. Finally I decided to retreat to the lower deck and settle near the coffin. After all, I couldn't offend the dead.

All night a group of women encircling the coffin sang as I was drenched by waves crashing over the side of the dangerously overloaded ship. Soaked and exhausted, I eventually climbed to the top deck where I found myself a wedge of floor space.

"It's wet there," warned a passenger.

"So?" I said. I was already wet.

"Where you put your mat," he explained, "you're next to the only men's bathroom. People have been drinking and . . . they miss."

Horrified, I grabbed my mat and contemplated my next move. It was late and the darkness was punctuated by choral snoring. After tiptoeing around the top deck, I finally found another spot, settled down, and as I unwrapped my sandwich, a palm-sized cockroach bolted across my legs. I dropped the food. Be calm, be centered, I told myself, and picked it up again. A roach the size of a regulation softball crawled onto the bread. I screamed.

A gentleman named Brodney approached me. "Do you need help?" he asked gently.

Pale and exhausted, I gazed at him, and, smiling sweetly, he offered me a large loincloth. Was I supposed to strip and put it on as a prelude to swinging from the ship's mast like Tarzan? I felt dumb and dumbfounded.

"Okay?" Brodney asked.

I raised one eyebrow.

Taking this to mean "yes," Brodney deftly twisted the loincloth into a hammock which he suspended from two nails. Then he helped me climb inside. At last I felt safe, and I closed my eyes. Suspended above the deck in a gently rocking loincloth, I would finally catch some winks. Five minutes later, the rains came—pelting thick ribbons of water that drenched me and Brodney's loincloth.

Fourteen hours after leaving Yap I arrived at Mog Mog, where I encountered topless girls in grass skirts and men wearing loincloths. Only the fourth outside visitor in a year, I was chided for changing my shoes on the steps of what turned out to be the sacred men's house. I hobbled across sharp stones until my feet bled. A few locals took pity on me and invited me to their outdoor cooking areas where they offered me fresh fish, tarot, stew, and as much coconut water as I could drink.

Eventually, I camped outside the house where the coffin lay amid the ritualized crying of grief-stricken women. As they wailed, they also expressed their feelings about the deceased—which were not always positive.

A man from Mog Mog who acted as my translator said mourners may talk about the generosity of the deceased and also his drinking and abusive behavior. They can praise his skills as a storyteller and regret his periodic irresponsibility and lying to cover up for his wrongdoing. They can lionize or lambaste him.

At first I was shocked. *Can't they just leave the dead in peace?* I wondered. But I said nothing, sitting and listening to the wailing and talk. And the more I thought about it, the more I began to understand. During a Mog Mog funeral, people are expected to air all of their feelings about the deceased person publicly, so the negative emotions don't fester. The bad feelings are expressed, rather than repressed, and then they are buried along with the body. At a funeral, people unleash their true feelings, but speaking ill of the deceased outside of this context is taboo. And it is forbidden to bad-mouth the dead person once he is lying in his final resting place.

"It's good," I said to the translator. "It was worth traveling on the Micronesia Spirit. I learned something important today."

He grinned and offered me one of two coconuts he had just climbed a palm tree to harvest. I looked around but there were no straws. He tossed his head back and sucked the coconut water from his fruit. I did the same. On Mog Mog, I quenched both my thirst and my curiosity. I had witnessed a very significant ceremony.

The funeral experience lingered with me for a long time. Perhaps the inhabitants of Mog Mog got it right. A person doesn't automatically ascend to sainthood just because he has left the earthly plane. Maybe honoring a person for what he did right or wrong during his lifetime isn't a bad idea. It may actually be inspired.

People are not perfect. They hurt others knowingly and unknowingly. Perhaps we can honor a person just by being truthful about him. We can allow him to be a human—with strengths and flaws, good behavior and bad.

I wondered if it would bother me if people said the truth about me after I left the earthly plane.

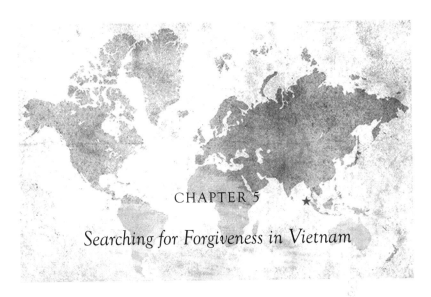

CHAPTER 5 ★

Searching for Forgiveness in Vietnam

I F YOUR BODY LIKES BEING WORKED ON, it will love being in Vietnam. And my recommendation is to go to places the locals frequent. You can get a face massage in a beauty shop; it lasts ninety minutes, costs less than a ticket to the movies, and involves an upper body massage, more washings and rinsings than you can shake a comb at, and, near the end, they shave your face with a straight-edge razor. It doesn't matter if you are male, female, or have facial hair. It's something you can talk about at cocktail parties for the rest of your life.

A whole body massage may entail soaking in red herbal liquid in a wooden tub, and since you are forewarned, you won't think you are bleeding to death. Afterwards, the masseur or masseuse will find and knead body parts you didn't even know you had. When was the last time you had your ear lobes or nostrils massaged?

I became addicted to these long, languorous, quirky body treatments, and I still laugh about them, but one particularly stands out in my mind: it was the time I reclined in a leather lounger in a communal room in a foot massage parlor in Hanoi. With me were three ex-Viet Cong guerrilla fighters from the Vietnam War; during the conflict, they were our officially-designated enemies. Now we all wore striped shorts that looked like prison issue, and we were groaning with pleasure and pain as our sore spots were massaged by young therapists.

As I lay there, I flashed back to the day, more than three decades before, when I left the U.S.A. because I was so angry and disturbed about the loss of young American lives and the millions of Vietnamese we had killed and maimed with our arsenals of weapons, defoliants, deceits, and disinformation.

I went to live in Paris, where negotiations were going on between America and Vietnam, and the anti-war protests were vigorous. I stayed out of the country for nine years—living in Europe and Africa—and have always been haunted by that war.

Two years ago, I finally went to Vietnam, driven by the necessity of finding out what had happened since then, and how they felt about Americans now. My guide, Cuong, had been a Viet Cong guerrilla fighter, and it was through him that I met ex-soldiers, Communist Party members, kids, and elders; he had set up the foot massage so I could hang with his old military cronies and find some answers to my questions.

"Are you angry about the war?" I asked my foot massage buddies, as our tootsies soaked in little tubs.

They gave me the same answer everyone had given me all over Vietnam.

"It's over."

"It was a long time ago."

"We welcome Americans."

"Sometimes, when we drink with our military buddies, we talk about the past. But then we come back to our daily lives. We don't forget the past and the war, but we don't think about it either. We look to the future."

"After the war, I hated anything with an American trademark. Now I like it. During the war, we saw distorted caricatures of bloodthirsty Americans in propaganda cartoons. Now when I meet Americans, I think they are so handsome and friendly."

"We have even met with American soldiers who came back here. They arrived full of guilt and some went to apologize in villages where they had killed people. We embraced them and we even cried together."

"Some of us still have bad memories and sometimes nightmares, but we don't suffer as much as the American G.I.s."

I turned away and a few tears coursed down my cheeks. There are several hundred thousand Vietnam veterans living on the streets of America. Purportedly, more committed suicide after the war than had died in combat. PTSD wrecks relationships and ruins lives. The conflict in Southeast Asia is an open wound on our national conscience. But in Vietnam, there's another story.

They welcome Americans, French, Japanese—all their former enemies—and look to the West for inspiration. The Communist Party still holds sway, but there is roaring free enterprise, a thriving stock market, open discussion and criticism of the party, and unstoppable individualism and ingenuity. Vietnam is high on the tourist radar because it is safe, beautiful, varied, modern, tribal, and exotic.

In Hanoi, where Ho Chi Minh once walked the streets in his rubber sandals and did strategic war planning, you can now shop, take a ride in a human-propelled *cyclo*, see a water puppet show, and watch break dancers. In the Gulf of Tonkin—where our government's bogus claims that an American ship was bombed became our excuse to enter the war—you can now cruise Halong Bay with its 1,969 spectacular sandstone islands. You can fly to Da Nang, once home to forty-five U.S. military bases, and have a custom wardrobe made in twenty-four hours in nearby Hoi An.

You can also go on the trail of the war, as I did. The infamous Hanoi Hilton prison is open for visits. There's a plaque marking the spot where John McCain's plane went down, and the wreckage of a B-52 bomber is still in Huu Tiep Lake in Hanoi. You can learn about what they refer to as "the American War" at the War Remnants Museum in Ho Chi Minh City (Saigon), and crawl through the claustrophobia-inducing tunnels at Cu Chi, where the fighters from the north conducted their guerrilla war against the American troops. They have even accommodated American visitors by enlarging the tunnels because the Vietnamese were and are so much smaller and thinner.

These tunnels were the only place I saw Cuong express strong emotion about the American War.

"I will not go inside with you," he said adamantly. "No way."

He had spent weeks in the earthen warrens, sharing space with rodents, starving, his body and soul gasping for air and light. He said he felt like a rat. Down at the third level of the caves, it was like Hades. "When you came out," he said, "it was like returning from Hell."

"Aren't you angry, Cuong, that our war forced you to live there?"

"Nope!" Cuong insisted. "But it's not a place I would ever want to visit again!"

And then he went on to describe a day when he was so famished he ran out of hiding and into a river where, with his bare hands, he grabbed two fish that had been killed or stunned as a result of bombing. At that moment, he was spotted by the U.S. military.

"The shells went off in front of me," Cuong said, "and I could hear whizzing and shredding. I dove underwater. I held my breath, waiting."

"What happened next?" I prodded him, totally caught up in his narrative.

"We knew the pattern of the enemy fire. I knew they would move thirty yards away, and, if I could just keep holding my breath, I would be safe."

"Sounds like a close call."

"Very," Cuong said, nodding. "And then it was over. They had moved on. I came up from the water and two buddies of mine stood there looking at me. They started to laugh. I had just escaped death, and why were they amused? Because after all of that, I emerged with the two fish still clutched in my hands. That's how hungry I was."

"Were you thinking about death all the time?" I asked Cuong.

"I read Epicurious," he said, and "one sentence really struck me. I made it my own. It was: 'Why worry about death?' When you are alive, it doesn't come. When it comes, you aren't conscious. So why worry about it? I told this to my war friends and it helped a lot when we were waiting for the enemy on the front."

"How have you managed to put the American War behind you?" I asked everyone I met. The answer was always the same. The Vietnamese are so happy not to be at war or under foreign occupation that they are concentrating on the present, on making money, and bettering themselves. Their focus is on the now and the future. The war represents the past.

"Do you mean you really have no resentment against us?" I asked again and again.

"No," was the answer. "You are forgiven."

It was an enormous relief to know that Vietnam has survived our war and is thriving. It was reassuring to learn that life has moved on, and even when a country is bombed, defoliated, and destroyed, it can come back with great vigor. I was humbled by a people who have suffered so much and have chosen forgiveness over fury.

One night, in a park in Hanoi, I met a silver-haired man dressed in beige pants, sandals, and a white, short-sleeve shirt. His grace suggested someone who had practiced Tai Chi for decades. In fact, he had been a Viet Cong soldier and then did menial labor most of his life. He spoke with the wisdom of a philosopher. "I was eaten up by anger when I was younger," he said. "So I spent many years meditating and thinking about anger and whom I was angry at. Were the soldiers who came here to fight any different from me? I didn't want to go to war. But, once I was forced to, I did whatever I had to do in order to survive. There was no difference between the American soldiers and me. We were both caught up in a situation and circumstances. When I realized that, I could give up my anger. Now, I think of those soldiers with compassion."

My guide, Cuong, chimed in. "I didn't want to go to war either. What did I know or care about Lenin and socialism at age eighteen? I wanted to stay home and play rock 'n' roll songs on my guitar. I loved the Beatles. I sang 'Let It Be.' I lived in the jungle, on the verge of starvation for five years with no news of my family. In my squad of twelve, only two of us survived. I have a scar from a grenade on my scalp. My leg was wounded. It wasn't the fault of the soldiers. Life is good now. Forget the past—I live in the present. After what I went through, I never take anything for granted. I appreciate everything, every little thing and each moment. I forgave the soldiers a long time ago."

Only once, in a remote Black Hmong village in the mountains in the north of Vietnam, did someone ask me a question about the American War. I was sitting on a bamboo floor, in a house on stilts, laughing with a woman named Mai and her family. Mai was a lithe woman who wore her hair in a knot—called a *tang cau*—on the left side of her head, which is the tradition for married women. Her children giggled as they rolled up my shirt sleeves and the legs of my pants to stare at my white skin. Mai chided them gently, but when she saw that I wasn't offended, she chuckled too. She served me tea, and, after I had inquired about her tribe and traditions, I invited her to ask me any questions she wished. Mai hesitated for a moment and looked over at a rifle which hung on the wall, a relic of the war in which her father had fought against the Americans. Then she asked, in a barely audible voice, "Why did the Americans come to my country during the war?"

My mind wandered to Iraq, Afghanistan, Pakistan, and Yemen, and I felt the same anger I had felt during the war in Vietnam. As we talked and exchanged ideas in a house on stilts, how many innocent civilians were dying? How many families were being wrecked and futures cut short in a burst of gunfire?

One day, when the insanity has stopped, when Iraq and Afghanistan finally know peace and have been rebuilt, will they, too, thrive? Will we be taking trips to Baghdad, Kabul, and Islamabad the way we now go to Ho Chi Minh City and Hanoi to see remnants and reminders of the war? Will guns hang on walls as decorative relics? Most important, will they be able to forgive us?

The fact that the Vietnamese can forgive Americans caused me to look at myself and how I feel about people who have hurt or offended me. There is one woman, an angry, misguided person, who, in the past, slandered me both privately and publicly, in writing. She caused a lot of pain and distress in my life. And, from what I heard, she was at it again.

I thought about retribution and how I could get back at her. I put my hands on my keyboard, ready to spew out a nasty, angry letter. I wanted to tell her that she was a blight on the face of the universe, a ball of negativity, a self-righteous, racist liar. Furthermore, that she used up too much air on the planet and created divisiveness everywhere she went. But before doing it, I stopped for a moment to consider my actions. And in an instant I realized that I didn't have to write the letter. In fact, I didn't need to do anything at all.

I got up and walked away from my computer. I understood that I could spend a lifetime harboring anger and resentment, or I could accept what happened to me and move on. It felt good to be in the present. It felt good not to focus on the past. It felt right to unplug from past hurts and bitterness. My trip to Vietnam inspired me and reminded me of that.

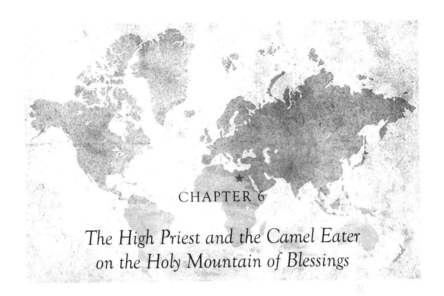

★

CHAPTER 6

The High Priest and the Camel Eater
on the Holy Mountain of Blessings

THERE ARE PLENTY OF THINGS I AM SCARED OF, but people usually don't intimidate me. As I travel the world, I've been fortunate to meet with ministers and mystics, rock stars, scientists, and shamans. I was never really nervous until the auspicious day when I was invited to a private audience with the High Priest of the ancient Israelite Samaritans. It was as though someone had opened the pages of the Torah or Hebrew Bible and invited me to step inside.

The Samaritans are northern Israelites whose deep tribal ancestry goes back to Joseph, the son of forefather Jacob and great grandson of Abraham. Today, more than 3,800 years later, they still pray at the site where Joseph's bones are said to be buried. The first High Priest was Aaron, the brother of Moses. The current High Priest, Elazar B. Tsedaka, traces his lineage back through 131 High Priests to Itamar, the second son of Aaron. Abraham. Joseph. Jacob. Moses. Aaron. You can begin to understand why I was a little skittish about an audience with a man of such prestige and pedigree.

Roughly half of the 729 Samaritans in the world live in Holon, a town south of Tel Aviv, and the other half live on the West Bank on *Har Gerizim*, the holy Mountain of Blessings mentioned in the Hebrew Bible. And there I was, standing on their mountain, heading toward the gate of the High Priest's house. Like all Samaritans, he had verses from the Torah inscribed outside his dwelling.

I was welcomed into a lavish Oriental-style living room. Moments later, the bearded High Priest entered, wearing a gray robe and red turban. A dignified man in his early eighties, he was accompanied by his family and his deputy High Priest, Aaron B. Ab-Hisda. He beckoned for me to sit next to him. The audience had begun.

"What can I do for you?" he inquired.

"You have an ancient tradition of Biblical interpretation and I wonder if I can ask a few questions," I said cautiously.

When he nodded, I dove in.

"I know the Samaritans consider Moses to be the greatest prophet who ever lived, but how did he convince the recalcitrant Israelites of his importance?" I asked.

"Moses could do many things," the High Priest explained. "He put his hand inside his shirt, and when he pulled it out, the hand had leprosy. Then he stuck it into his shirt again, and it came out clean."

"What about the five Hebrew words Moses used to cure his sister Miriam of leprosy?" I asked excitedly. "I've thought about those words many, many times. Would you agree they can be used for healing?"

He nodded.

"And is it true that the words mean 'Please, God, heal her, please,' but they can be used to heal a man as well?"

"Yes," he replied. "The words of the Torah cannot be changed. So they're used for men as well as women. Also, healing takes place in the soul, which is feminine. For those reasons, the words pertain to men as well as women."

High Priest Elazar proceeded to give me a rather complex numerological analysis of the five words. Apparently, he had also thought about Moses's healing words many, many times. It created a bond between us. The High Priest thanked me for asking such meaningful questions. He became less formal. Friendly, actually. I pinched myself. There I was, on chatty terms with the revered icon.

He mused about Abraham, Isaac, Jacob. He explained that Israelite Samaritans cover their faces when they say the names of the forefathers, because they are so holy. He gently ran his open hand, palm facing inward, over his eyes to illustrate what he meant. I was hyperventilating with excitement. I felt as though time dissolved and I was in the desert, engaging with someone from the family of Moses.

He spoke about the revered matriarchs of the Bible, the ten plagues, and the golden calf. He made the events seem as though they had happened yesterday or perhaps a few years ago. We chitchatted about Joseph's dream interpretations, Noah's ark, and Lot's wife who looked back when she should have looked forward. In the course of our conversation, he mentioned something about a camel.

"Ah, camel," I said. "I once ate one in a Bedouin tent. It was tasty, actually."

The High Priest stiffened. He set his jaw.

"You ate camel?" he asked me, incredulous.

"Sure. I guess you could say it was like very tender roast beef. Soft and succulent. A bit of a meaty tang. You should try it sometime if you get tired of chicken," I joked.

The color drained from the High Priest's face. It drained from the face of the deputy High Priest. It drained from the faces of the High Priest's family.

"You ate *camel?*" the High Priest repeated. The words bounced off the walls and slapped me in the face.

"I shouldn't have eaten camel?" I asked in a small, insecure, parched voice.

"Eating camel is worse than eating pig!" pronounced the religious potentate.

It was at this moment I knew I had crossed a line. I wasn't sure where the line was, but I was on the other side of it. The Samaritans are all extremely observant and one hundred percent kosher. They won't even eat certified kosher food outside of their homes in Israel or America because it's not kosher enough.

"I didn't eat a lot of it," I said, trying to backtrack. "Maybe half a camel steak. Probably more like a third. I'm sure I didn't even like it. I left a lot of it on my plate. I just pushed it around with my fork and sort of pretended I was eating it. Now that I think back, I probably spit it out."

The High Priest shook his head. I heard him talking about penitence—that I would have to do something to atone. I looked around the room, drowning in a sea of disapproval.

I fumbled inside my beige leather bag and extracted my see-through wallet. All eyes were on me. I rifled through my money and came to a bill that was given to me for luck during a classical opera in North Vietnam.

"Please, take this," I said, proffering the bill. "It has brought me a lot of good fortune. Now it's yours."

"Thank you," he said. "I have a coin collection and this is a good addition." I am sure he thought I was nuts. A consumer of camel handing him a Vietnamese dong note to atone.

"Sir, I just want to say that . . . well . . . I won't eat camel again. The next time it's offered to me, I'll pass. I promise."

The High Priest nodded, but our intimacy was gone. I had blown it. Over a hump-backed steak in a Bedouin tent. I had insulted my host with my gut. I was a culinary criminal in his eyes.

And then, just when I was deflated enough to skulk out of the room, the High Priest smiled. "It has been very enjoyable talking Torah with . . . with . . . a camel eater," he said.

"Please, sir," I answered, "a repentant camel eater."

He laughed. I laughed. The deputy High Priest laughed. The family laughed. Soon we were all cackling. After I left, I heard that the High Priest asked how the camel eater was, and if she had gotten home safely. I suppose that meant that he couldn't forget my sin, but he was able to forgive me.

He was a wise man, the High Priest Elazar. He taught me that I can unwittingly screw up and commit a cultural faux pas out of ignorance. I can offend someone's sensibilities by what I say, the clothes I wear, and even by what I eat. But it takes a man of substance, of wisdom, to leapfrog over condemnation to compassion.

Recently, I was in a restaurant in Santa Fe, New Mexico. A waiter was fuming because he had spent a lot of time helping two young foreigners understand the menu and order. He had even brought them free *sopapillas* and honey to dip them in. Then he had advised them on where they could go for a hike. When they exited the restaurant, they had not left a tip.

I immediately thought about the High Priest and decided to speak to the offended waiter. I told him I sympathized with him, and suggested that maybe in the young men's country, tips were not the norm. He spewed out a cranky epithet or two and then shrugged and said maybe that was true. I heard him tell the woman who worked the cash register that he had been stiffed, and then he added, "Maybe in their country they don't give tips."

I smiled inwardly. The waiter did exactly what my role model in a turban did on the Mountain of Blessings. He was insulted, but he chalked it up to a cultural miscalculation, and forgave it.

As I write these words, I have learned that the High Priest just passed on. I am honored that I got to meet and spend time with him. I was feeling very sad about his death when I received an email from my dear Samaritan friend Benny Tsedaka. He, too, was sad, but he closed his missive by saying that "We all must pass. Only God is Eternal."

CHAPTER 7

In a Mexican Prison

CHETUMAL, IN THE SOUTHERN YUCATAN PENINSULA IN MEXICO, just a few hours away from the international playground of Cancún, is where I went to prison. I was able to gain entrance because I collect prison art. You are probably wondering why I collect prison art and why I wanted to enter the prison. There is a long answer and a short one. The latter seems most appropriate here.

I have never really been interested in the mainstream. Actually, most people are fascinated by the mainstream, so the mainstream doesn't need my interest. What makes my ticker beat faster is discovering voices, people, places, realities that are not generally known. And serious offenders fall into that category. The stories of how and why they descended into the bowels of crime make great films and books but, in real life, the general feeling is that convicted criminals are monsters and they should be locked up and punished.

This would be fine if it worked. The perps would learn their harsh lessons out of sight of the rest of us. But, as we all know, one day the prison gates open and the perp is free. If he and we are lucky, he has had a change of heart, and he becomes a productive member of society. If he has learned little inside the prison except how to be a better criminal, then nothing has been gained and plenty has been lost. In fact, we are all the losers.

Behind every criminal face is a human who once was a bouncing baby, gurgling with glee, and aching to be loved. Then, something happened. Each story is different, provocative, sad, and disturbing. Needs were denied or not met, the environment was violent or cruel or indifferent, and feelings with no healthy outlets were expressed in unspeakable acts. I learned this when I volunteered for six years in a juvenile detention facility, and I spent time with some baby-faced serious offenders who were shockingly young and others who had already logged years in a life of crime and were on their way to chronic criminality and incarceration.

Beneath the machismo, the drugs, the gangs, there are human beings who—although they no longer gurgle with glee—are often still capable of love, passion, pain, remorse, and creative output. In the detention facility I met frightening thugs who wrote tender, sensitive poems and created imaginative, highly expressive art.

Courts, judges, juries, and innocent victims are much more capable than I of dealing with issues of guilt, judgment, and sentencing. What interests me is getting a glimpse into a criminal's heart and finding a place, however tiny, where there is authentic feeling and sensitivity. To my mind, this is where hope for healing, rehabilitation, and redemption lie.

We all know that prisons are most often like the dark nights of the soul—rife with pain, hurt, rage, humiliation, isolation, revenge, and desperation. But believe me when I tell you that rays of enlightenment shone on that medium-security prison in Chetumal. It started at the top and trickled down to all those who are incarcerated.

The prison director, Victor Terrazas Cervera, walked around the garden-like inner courtyard of the prison unarmed, in shirtsleeves. He stopped to play with the prison's pet coatimundi (which looks like a cross between a raccoon and an anteater), and chatted with inmates, all of whom wore street clothes.

"Aren't you concerned about violence?" I asked Victor.

He grinned and answered, "There is none."

"This is a prison. You have serious offenders. There have to be incidents of violence."

"I can assure you that there hasn't been any violence in ten years."

He led me to a small, two-room arts and crafts shop. The bare, cracked, white walls were covered with paintings; mobiles hung from the ceiling; sculptures, wearable art, and jewelry were perched on rough-hewn shelves; and brightly-colored hammocks were displayed on wooden looms. All of the work was made by inmates.

A few of the incarcerated artists were milling about the shop, anxious to make contact and talk about their work. One of them held up a Ferris wheel fabricated from pieces of scrap metal and Coke cans, another proffered a Maya-themed painting, and a third was the proud artist who had produced a bracelet fashioned from large, chunky beads. A shy man, who looked down, stood next to two hand-woven purple and blue hammocks which he was selling for $50 each.

"In New York, that hammock would cost you $125," said the shy man's friend, who was also an artist. He pointed out his latest work: a papier-maché sculpture of a vintage, single-engine plane.

The buildings were run down, but the prisoners were pumped up. They made and sold multi-hued hammocks, wooden furniture, jewelry, picture frames crafted from plastic sleeves on soda bottles, and inventive toys. They took art workshops and sold their creations to the public in the small gift shop I visited. A few of the finer artists were even provided with their own studios.

On the grounds of the prison were a massage room (where very inexpensive Reiki and Swedish treatments were available) for physical stress, garden areas for meditation to relieve mental and emotional stress, and, for one dollar, inmates could spend a night with a spouse or partner in an on-site love motel—as long as they brought their own bedding and TVs or DVD players if they wished to use them. In the morning, they were required to leave the room in the condition they found it in.

"I think the conjugal visits—which are legally permitted in Mexico—help to prevent violence by releasing pent-up sexual tension," Victor explained, adding, "There are children conceived and born here when both parents are inmates; they raise the kids together. Many prisoners have families who come to visit them and we provide a playground area. One of the inmates is a clown, and he performs on Sundays."

Prisoners had access to a well-stocked library and could take classes in IT, Spanish, English, and even French and Japanese. They played soccer and belonged to sports teams. There were AA meetings and inmates were encouraged to pursue whatever interests they had so that they could develop skills and seek employment when they were released. When there was lingering anger or resentment between two prisoners, they were given padding and put in a boxing ring to duke it out. By the second round, they were often so worn out that they just shook hands or hugged and put their differences behind them.

Terrazas Cervera considered the inmates as human beings who had made mistakes in their lives and were capable of redemption. He treated them with the humanity and kindness many of them have never known before. He encouraged their creative self-expression and helped them to maintain dignity and self-respect by living in a community setting.

"It's just like a pueblo—a little city here," the unassuming director stated.

Although I would venture a guess that none of the prisoners enjoyed being incarcerated, if they had a choice they would probably opt for the facility in Chetumal. It seemed lax and laissez-faire on the surface, but there was a constant demand on the inmates: they were given every chance to grow, change, and be rehabilitated. They were expected to function as a community. If they behaved like human beings, they would be treated that way. They were invited to be the best they could be—a radical shift from their previous lives. They were not coddled. They were exposed to communal values and norms and encouraged to develop the positive sides of their personalities.

The second time I went to the prison, I took twenty-seven adult journalism students with me. Some were lawyers, teachers, scientists, accountants. I wondered what they would think and how they would react. At first they were apprehensive, but within minutes they were talking with inmates, taking photos, buying art.

"Of all the wondrous things I saw in Mexico," one of them told me, "this is the place that moved me most. It completely changed the way I think about prisons, prisoners, and rehabilitation."

Another student cradled a foot-high wooden sculpture of a sensuous, voluptuous woman that she had just purchased.

At home, I smile every time I open my closet and see a large, brightly-colored purse made from the foil shrink wrapping from plastic soda bottles. I bought it for $20 at the prison, and I can still see the beaming, round face of the man who sold it to me. Victor told me the money would help feed his family, so I got a purse and a good feeling for a few dollars.

My experience in Mexico greatly influenced how I think about crimes and punishment.

For many years, I have corresponded with Raphael (not his real name), a Mexican national incarcerated in the southwestern U.S. He was convicted of a violent crime and has affiliations in prison that he refuses to renounce. Rafael spends every day and every night in isolation, only leaving his depressing and claustrophobic cell for about an hour to go to the yard.

I am constantly agog at Rafael's brilliance. He has taught himself English and writes with the fluency of a native speaker. He is a philosopher, artist, and poet. The verse he writes is so powerful and authentic that my friend Nancy collected and published it in a book.

The only thing I didn't like about Rafael was that he was homophobic and harbored prejudice against black people; Hispanic and black people are at odds in the facility where he lives.

I decided to try a bit of Victor's philosophy. I asked a gay friend named Artemes, who is a singer and actor, and an African American friend if they would be willing to write to Rafael. Both said yes. Artemes and Rafael have developed such a deep relationship that it can easily be called love. They admire, respect, and fantasize about each other. And ever since Rafael started writing to my African American friend, he has dropped all hostility and judgment of the latter's race. He has stopped generalizing about groups of people and shows gratitude to his correspondents by sending them cards, drawings, and poems.

In my opinion, Rafael is totally rehabilitated. His head is full of dreams of the future now and his writing is laced with hope, compassion for his guards, and clear thinking about what landed him in prison, and how he will never make those destructive life choices again.

Rafael grew up surrounded by violence. He was never exposed to healthy, peaceful human interactions. In prison he encountered rage, racism, confinement, sadism, and squalid conditions. But because people on the outside treated him kindly, believed in him, wrote to him, published his work, nurtured him, I feel fully confident that he can return to society and contribute to it. It's just a matter of when he gets released.

Treating prisoners as human beings, encouraging their skills, their intelligence, their creativity, can help to reduce the horrendous problem of violence and recidivism in our prisons.

This is not idealistic, pie-in-the-sky thinking. It's real. It's happened with Rafael. And it's happening right now in that little known Mexican prison.

CHAPTER 8

Meeting Maximon in Guatemala

I VIVIDLY RECALL THE FIRST TIME I SAW HIM IN GUATEMALA. He was sitting on a chair in a native marketplace, dressed in a black suit, black shoes, and a black hat. His mouth was open, pursed into a small "o." He was appealing, but also had a streak of danger about him.

"Who is he?" I asked a new Guatemalan friend.

"Maximon," she answered, pronouncing it mah-she-mone.

The second time, it was a hot, humid day, and I was looking for a grocery store to buy a bottle of water. He was in a shop which sold masks and textiles. I looked away and then I looked back at him. He was clearly staring at me.

"I see you like him," said the shopkeeper.

I nodded tentatively.

"Here," he said, and he handed Maximon and his chair to me. You see, Maximon was less than a foot high, and he was made of wood.

"Would you like to have him?"

I opened my wallet and then hesitated.

"I'm . . . not sure."

"He may not be here later," said the shopkeeper.

"Well . . . I'll have to take that chance. I can't really decide now."

The third time, he was sitting in a room in the home of a Maya healer named José. José was a member of a *cofradía*, or religious brotherhood, and Maximon occupied the place of honor on an altar flanked by two Christ figures. He wore the same black, European garb, but he was also adorned with colorful textiles, and there were bottles of aguardiente at his feet. He had a big, unlit cigar in his mouth.

"Can you tell me about him, please," I whispered to a Guatemalan man who had come for a healing.

"He's a god, but he likes to smoke and drink like the rest of us."

It was hard for me to understand this. A wooden god who smokes and drinks?

"Where does he come from?" I asked the man.

"Santiago Atitlán," he answered, and so I went there.

Lake Atitlán is one of the jewels of Guatemala—a spectacular expanse of deep, blue water surrounded by three majestic, looming volcanoes: Toliman, Atitlán, and San Pedro. I took a boat to Santiago, a Maya village at an altitude of over 5,000 feet. Guided by a seven- or eight-year-old girl in worn and faded clothes, I wandered through hilly streets that were paved with uneven stones.

The young girl didn't speak much, but focused on her task of getting me to a Maximon shrine. After about twenty minutes, she stopped in front of a low, cement house and gestured for me to go in. When I entered, I was not alone. There, in a small room, was a life-sized Maximon, and near him was his guardian, a member of the brotherhood of the Holy Cross. The guardian waved an incense burner made from an old coffee tin with punctured holes, filling the room with ribbons of copal smoke.

On cement benches that lined the wall facing Maximon, Maya people waited patiently and whispered in their K'iche' language. When it was their turn, they made a cash offering of quetzals (Guatemalan currency), burned candles (different colors represent different favors that are requested), put cigarettes in Maximon's mouth, and donated small bottles of alcohol. Some of the alcohol was poured into Maximon's rigid, open mouth, and when the liquor began to dribble, the guardian lovingly mopped up the figure's chin and neck.

A guide entered the room with a few Japanese visitors in tow, and we began to speak. He told me that Maximon is revered by Maya and many other people, and he may be the reincarnation of Maam, an ancient Maya god of the underworld. His name may come from this god, or perhaps it derives from "*max*," which means "tobacco" in the Maya language. Alternately, his name may signify "bound with string or rope."

More people arrived, offering more candles, more to drink, more to smoke—single cigars and cigarettes or whole boxes. The atmosphere got noisy, hazy, permeated with the smell of alcohol. The more people I questioned about Maximon, the more confused I became. He was a saint. A devil. The godfather or grandfather of the village who protected the inhabitants from evil and witches. A doctor. A trickster. A potent miracle worker and healer. An ancient Maya god synchretized with San Simon, or, perhaps, Judas Iscariot. A Maya leader who was hitched to a chair and burned by the Spanish in the middle of the sixteenth century. Pedro de Alvarado, the brutal conquistador who ravaged the Maya culture and people.

Maya supplicants bowed low in front of Maximon or got down on their knees praying. They implored him for food, health for a family member, crops, a safe voyage, success at selling in the market. Red candles were lit for love, white to protect the children, pink for health, and yellow for the elders. Some people spoke briefly, some for a long time. To them, Maximon was not a wooden figure—he was holy, someone in whom they believed, a miracle maker, a granter-of-wishes, an intimate god they could turn to in times of need.

"Did you make a donation and request something?" a woman asked me.

"I don't have quetzales," I replied.

"Maximon takes dollars too."

I reached into my wallet, but I hesitated, as I had done in the store. I wasn't ready to make an offering to Maximon because I didn't really understand him. And then a man from Guatemala City came into the room. His English was almost perfect, he worked as a guide, and he had a Canadian couple in tow.

I listened carefully as he told them about Maximon.

"He is a divinity, but one who is very revered because he understands human vice and sin. He enjoys smoking, drinking, and carousing, just like people do."

"Why do they worship someone like that?" asked the Canadian man.

"He forgives and offers hope to people, even to those who have done desperate or terrible things," he answered. "Because he himself is a sinner, he is able to forgive."

It was precisely the information I'd hoped for. Like every other human, I had done things wrong. Acted thoughtlessly. Missed opportunities when I could have done better. I had asked The Big One in the sky to excuse me, I had felt bad, guilty, remorseful over the course of my life. But I never had a chance to request absolution from a god with alcohol dribbling down his chin and rolled tobacco protruding from his mouth. I placed money in the offering box, lit a candle, and looked at Maximon. "I am sorry for anything I have ever done wrong," I told him. "Can I sort of ask for global absolution instead of enumerating every petty error of the past?"

I looked up. Was it possible? I saw a twinkle in Maximon's right eye, and I somehow knew I was forgiven, and I could go forward with a clean slate in life.

"Enjoy your booze and cigarettes," I told him, as I exited the room. And I walked into the sunny outdoors, feeling like a better, lighter, happier person.

It didn't take long to have a Maximon-induced experience in my own life. I have a friend who drinks, pops pills and has done a dance of death with heroin for years. He has been on and off the horse more times than a Pony Express rider. He recently told me about a serious relapse, and as he lacerated himself for his weakness, his worthlessness, and how he disappointed everyone around him, his eyes filled with tears.

I told him about the wooden god in Guatemala who drank and smoked, and how I learned in his shrine that perfection is a crazy dream, an ill-conceived illusion. To inhabit a human body is to be imperfect.

My friend looked at me and said, "There is a little voice that worms its way into my mind every time I give it space. It says 'you are not good enough' so often that I have come to believe it. I'm always comparing myself to others, and they always seem to be more productive and successful than I am."

"Maximon thinks all of that is cabbage!" I said. It came out of me so suddenly that I was surprised. "You have vices and so does he. He accepts people the way they are: imperfect, trying their best but not always succeeding. I can understand why he's a god in the Guatemalan pantheon. He's willing to help anyone who asks him, without judgment. He's not holier than thou and he doesn't hold up a standard humans can't achieve."

My friend exploded in laughter. "Maybe I should keep my eye out for Maximon the next time I'm in a bar," he said. "He'll probably order a whiskey and light up a Cuban cigar."

I recently heard that my friend has sworn off drinking and using again. Far away in Guatemala, Maximon, who is certainly swilling, is also smiling. And if this little-known god can forgive human error, I'm willing to wager that whatever God you pray to can too.

CHAPTER 9

The Sorceress's Apprentice in Mexico

I T'S CALLED "LA TIERRA DE BRUJOS"—the land of the witches. Juventino Rosas, a traditional agricultural town in Guanajuato state in Central Mexico, has a reputation for being home to good witches, bad witches, and folk healers. What all three have in common is that they work with energy—the unseen force that keeps every living thing functioning and connects all entities to each other. This energy goes by other names in different cultures, like chi, prana, or life force. Without energy, you and I would be big blobs of dead matter.

The special power of *brujos* enables them to read, interpret, manipulate, and move energy. When something is amiss in an individual—physically, emotionally, or spiritually—the energy is thought to be blocked, and a powerful brujo knows how to move it.

The brujo tradition is handed down from parent to child or from teacher to student. Sometimes a brujo is self-taught; he or she gets a dream, a message, or a mysterious transmission of information about how to heal. And of course, as with any other profession, there are really gifted brujos and run-of-the-mill or even bogus brujos. Some are world-famous and others are only known to family, friends, and folks in the neighborhood.

Some witches are born with special aptitudes, as though their life mission is to be a brujo. But for those without the initial witchy spark, the techniques can also be taught.

Because energy work is so potent, it can be used for good or nefarious purposes: it can heal or it can harm. But it is only the healing that interests me, and I never bothered to find out much about the latter.

To be honest, saying that healing interests me is a gross understatement. It is a great, driving passion in my life.

My great-grandmother was a healer in a Russian *shtetl*, or village, and she did diagnosis by melting wax over a fire, molding it into a ball, and gazing into it. When she got a vision, she knew what to do to help the ailing person. Maybe it's in my genes. Perhaps one day I'll melt a candle and see a vision in wax. But, in the meantime, when I travel the world as a journalist, I track down indigenous healers and healing modalities that are rapidly disappearing. I don't interview them to find out what they do and how they do it; that would be like asking Lance Armstrong to describe his cycling or Aretha to explain her singing. I request a private session so I can experience firsthand what each healer does. In most cases, they allow their work to be photographed and videotaped. I never take this for granted and am always grateful.

Eight years ago, when I was in Guanajuato state on assignment, I heard about the town of Juventino Rosas. It took several hours on a chicken bus to get there, and when I arrived, I asked a taxi driver who the best local healer was. I was directed to the home of Ana Maria de Vilar.

Arriving at the home of a healer is often an experience with ritualized frustration. This time was no different. I stood outside an iron gate for about fifteen minutes, alternately knocking and cowering from the ferocious barking of an unseen dog. Finally, a woman who seemed to be in her thirties walked slowly up to the gate.

"What do you want?" she asked, looking me up and down.

"I would like a *limpia*," I said. I knew a bit about the Mexican tradition and understood that a limpia was supposed to clear or cleanse the energy field and get rid of negative influences.

Without another word, the woman disappeared. I waited another five minutes until she came back, opened the gate, and accompanied me into the healer's house. A few minutes later, her mother, Ana, appeared. A plump, middle-aged Mexican *curandera* (healer), she wore a floral housedress and oversized glasses and had a warm, gentle, earth-mother kind of face. "What do you want?" she asked me.

"I would like a limpia," I repeated.

"You will have to come back in three days," Ana informed me.

Three days?! I thought. *I just spent hours getting here on a chicken bus. I have to go back to my hotel and chicken-bus it back here in three days? Is she kidding?* This is what I thought, but what I said was, "Yes, I will come back in three days."

This has happened almost every time I've schlepped into the mountains, climbed down into valleys, or trekked through the jungle to find a healer. When I've found him or her, I've been told to come back several days later. I suppose it is some kind of initiation rite to separate the merely-curious from the seriously-intentioned.

That night, back at my hotel, after dusting myself off from the chicken bus which I had shared with fifteen cement bags, I had a strange dream. In it was the word "*serpiente.*" I was surprised to have a Spanish word pop into my nocturnal ramblings.

Three days later, as instructed, I arrived back at Juventino Rosas and went directly to Ana's house. This time there was almost no waiting. Ana led me into her private chapel, or *capilla*, which was adjacent to her house. It was a rectangular-shaped room lined with beautiful, old, wooden Mexican string instruments, images and statues of Jesus, and many candles. Ana beckoned me to stand on a large, inlaid stone cross. She burned *copal* (an aromatic tree resin) over smoldering coals in a ceramic *incensario* and smoke filled the capilla. Instinctively I closed my eyes as Ana circled me and performed the limpia, waving herbs in the air and intoning a deep, heartfelt prayer.

Afterwards, I told her that I'd had a dream where the word "serpiente" appeared. She burst into tears. I had no idea what I had done, but I was sorry I had done it.

Ana summoned her two daughters. She said something about "serpiente" to them, and they also began to cry. I stood there watching them cry. "*Lo siento,*" I said, "I am really sorry."

Ana reached out, patted me on my shoulder, and somehow I was able to understand that her husband, Pedro, had been a famous healer, and he had died a year and a half before. They were waiting for a sign from him, and that sign was the serpiente—the snake. Still crying, Ana went back into the capilla and emerged with a large, carved, wooden rain stick in the form of a snake. She presented it to me and insisted I take it. She said it was used to bring down the power of the moon during healings.

"We are connected forever," Ana told me. "One day you will work with me as my assistant."

And so there I was, six years later, at the Leon airport, looking around for a cab to take me back to Juventino Rosas. Someone called my name; I spun around, and was surprised to see Ana. Although she was in her late sixties and had serious health issues, she'd been standing there for three hours waiting to fetch her assistant. Ushering me into a cab, she insisted on paying, and we drove to her large, sprawling house.

Ana shared her home with eleven family members, and trying to understand Spanish with everyone talking at the same time was exhausting. I assumed that I would be sleeping on a couch in the television room, with no privacy or quiet time, but one of Ana's daughters generously gave up her bedroom for me.

At ten A.M., every day, Ana received clients, many of whom had traveled hours to get there. Ana informed each client that I was her assistant, and every time she said it, I felt a wave of unreality tinged with fear. What in the world was I doing in a capilla in Central Mexico?

Each person or family group sat on a wooden bench in the capilla opposite Ana, who was on a chair. They spoke openly about their problems, which were a varied and complex combination of physical, psychological, emotional, and spiritual symptoms. They ranged from drug addiction to a swollen arm that didn't respond to medical treatment; from deep depression to headaches to stomach pain to rage at a cheating spouse.

Ana's face was expressionless, professional and unjudgmental as she asked questions. Some of the clients were quite ill, and they had consulted with witches who had told them not to go to doctors.

Ana leaned over and whispered to me, "I need to give them permission to go to medical experts. It's essential for their health."

Often, Ana prescribed herbal drinks, herbal baths, and footbaths with ingredients like sarsaparilla, dandelion, and horsetail.

For many clients, Ana performed a limpia, as she had done for me, but this time she told me the names of the main herbs she used: sweet basil and pepper tree. She ran raw eggs over the bodies of a few, and showed me how to "read" the egg as she cracked it and plopped its contents into a glass of water. The way the yoke fell and the degree of cloudiness of the egg white were clues about a person's state of health. Sometimes Ana burned little handmade candles, called "*velas*," and each one represented different aspects of Jesus, saints, portals to the spiritual world, the clients, and others who were causing them problems. Often the diagnosis was "*envidia*"—someone was envious of the client, or sending bad energy. A limpia would help to remove that bad juju. Ana told her clients that she sometimes effected miraculous cures and healed physical ailments. But the body and soul are intertwined and often required healing on both the physical and spiritual planes. Her expertise was the spiritual.

One day, in between clients, Ana pulled out a shoebox full of black, red, and green candles. "You need to know about these," she informed me.

"Ana . . . are these . . . are these . . . ?" I began, with a sense of foreboding.

"Yes, they are used for black magic," she said.

"I'm not interested," I protested.

"It is important," she said.

"I can live a long and happy life without knowing anything about black magic."

"This is part of your training."

She calmly explained to me that it was essential for me to understand the objects. Although she, Ana, only practiced healing and white witchcraft, there were many practitioners of the black arts, and these were some of their tools. They cast spells, were able to hurt people physically and psychically, and they dealt with the devil.

"Why would anyone want to hurt someone else?" I asked.

"Because the dark forces are very powerful," Ana replied. "People have been hurt or rejected by others, and they want to hurt them back. They pay a lot of money to witches for this. My husband Pedro, who learned his *curanderismo* from his Aztec and Chichimec ancestors and taught it to me, told me that you either work with God and forces of light or forces of darkness. You can't do both. Some witches practice both, but I don't. Like Pedro, I have chosen my way."

Ana led me over to a shelf in the capilla and showed me old peso notes that were singed and burned.

"This came from a witch who practiced the dark arts," she said. "She came into my capilla for a consultation and left me some money. When she had departed, the money spontaneously burst into flames."

Then Ana went to another shelf with envelopes that were stuffed with hundreds of photos. People had sent them from around the world so she could practice long-distance healing.

"This is my way," she said. "I pray for them."

My job in the capilla varied according to the client. Sometimes I handed Ana the incense burner or brought her the incense. Often I just sat next to her and she instructed me about the candles, the eggs, the incense, the herbs, or prayers.

One night, when the family was watching TV, I asked Ana why she didn't use a snake rain stick for healing. She confessed that since she had given hers to me six years before, she never got a new one. The next day, I took a bus to a nearby town and trekked from shop to shop, searching to no avail for a replacement rain stick. As night fell, I visited one last shop and there it was. When I gave it to Ana, I expressed a wish to learn how to use it to pull down the power of the moon. Ana grew silent. I dropped the subject.

For one week, I was in a constant state of overload and mental exhaustion from the language difficulty, but on the eighth day, there was a linguistic miracle: at six A.M. I awoke suddenly able to understand about seventy per-

cent of what was going on. (Speaking, however, was still difficult.) At seven
A.M., Ana announced I was going on a trip with her. A taxi was waiting in
front of the door. We got in, and it was not until we reached the outskirts
of Juventino Rosas that Ana said she was taking me to some sacred places
for healers and witches. I laughed and said I was ready for the Witch Tour.

For about an hour we rode towards San Miguel de Allende, finally
stopping at Santa Cruz de Puerto Calderón. "This is one of the sacred
portals," Ana explained, walking us into a small chapel where we were
greeted by a curandera. The woman had sad, sad eyes and was draped in
a *serape*. Four years before, the holy cross in the chapel, which had been
there since 1531, was stolen. The woman said she hadn't been able to
sleep, drink, or eat normally since. She told us that the cross came from
a time when the Indians were at war with the Spanish conquerors. There
was an awful battle nearby, with thousands of Indian and Spanish dead
on the battlefield. After the battle, the Indians saw the apparition of a
holy cross in the sky, and they understood the power of the religion to
which the Spanish had tried to forcibly convert them. They set up the
cross as a shrine and eventually a capilla was built there.

We got back into the cab and drove to a bridge on the old road to
San Miguel de Allende. Ana told the driver to stop, and instructed me to
climb down the steep, slippery, rocky path that led under the bridge. I did
as I was told and saw the candles and paraphernalia of black witchcraft.
The rocks had been charred black from smoke and candle-burning. And
there were remnants of food on paper plates.

"What is the food for?" I asked Ana as I climbed back into the cab.
"Is it an offering to the devil?"

She looked at me like I was stupid. "It's food. To eat. Witches who
work their spells get hungry too."

As we drove on, Ana explained that at every site where black witchcraft was performed, white witchcraft was also practiced. "They are holy
power spots, and can be used for good or evil intent," she said. "The
energy in these places is very intense, and can be used for healing or for
harm. Pedro and I have brought flowers and done limpias to cleanse the
bad energy from these power spots."

Ana turned to look at me in the back seat. "We're going to the village of Llanito now, and I need you to really pay attention," she said forcefully. "There will be an all-night vigil and fiesta there on New Year's Eve, and you must attend. All the Indians come, and pilgrims come, and many witches. You must stay up all night, and I will show you what to look for."

I got cold feet. Literally. It was extremely windy and cold in the tiny, nondescript, dusty, run-down village of Llanito. I became panicky at the thought of being there all night on December 31st alone—without a car or a place to rest and with limited Spanish. "Ana, I don't think I can get here again. I'll be staying in San Miguel de Allende after I leave your house. I have no transportation, no warm clothes, and I'm too paranoid to eat from roadside stands. I'll be tired and cold and hungry. I don't think I can do it. Will you be here?" I asked.

"No. I can't come this year. You will be here."

Damn, I thought. *Damn. I just can't do it.*

Ana took me into a small chapel in the church called El Señor de los Afligidos—our Lord of the Afflicted. She prayed in front of the Christ at the altar and pointed out that she had the same image of Christ in her own capilla. I nodded. I followed her around like a little *perro.* Then she instructed the cab driver to take us to three different *calvarios,* stone altars or shrines with niches inside. In each niche, she pointed out white candles that had been used by curanderos for healing and well-being. Then she pointed out black candles, black wax skulls, and miniature votives for harming children.

"Children?" I asked. "What sickos set out to hurt children?"

"If they can't get to the parents, they go after their children," she answered solemnly.

The cab driver ran away, spooked.

"You must know to recognize these things," Ana said to me, "so you can deflect their energy, and not let them harm you."

On the morning of the tenth day of living with Ana, I felt that I should not impose on the family any longer. I was packing my belongings, preparing to return the bedroom to Ana's daughter, and I was just about to call a cab to take me to the bus station when Ana's daughter came running in. "Ana needs you in the capilla—now," she insisted.

I dropped everything and ran into the capilla. Ana was with clients—a couple and a baby—and so I sat next to her and listened. The baby had been sick, the wife had been sick, and the man felt that perhaps he had been "witched" by his ex-wife who was envious of his newfound happiness. Ana lit candles, watched them melt, and told the man he was right. "*Envidia*," she said with certainty. Envy.

Then Ana turned to me and said she wanted *me* to work with the couple. I was totally, completely unprepared. "*Sola?*" I asked. Yes, she nodded. I stood up and walked to the altar, beckoning the couple to stand on the stone inlaid cross. I felt like an idiot. I knew nothing. Worse, I couldn't open my mouth and pray to Jesus in Spanish. I just couldn't do it. I looked imploringly at Ana. She smiled. I opened my mouth, and broken Hebrew came spilling out. I was cringing with embarrassment but no one said anything—not the couple and not Ana. I intoned what I remembered of an ancient Israelite prayer for healing. I was sweating down to my internal organs.

After the couple left, I was headed back to the bedroom to pack, when Ana pulled at my sleeve. She led me into an open courtyard behind her house, and held up the rain stick I had bought her.

"Now," she said, "the time has come. First I had to prepare the rain stick for use in the capilla, and I couldn't teach you until that was done. Now you'll learn to call down the power of the moon."

She showed me once, and then asked me to try. I held the rain stick upside down, I turned it right side up. I fumbled and felt like a fool. "If I ever try this, the moon will laugh at me and certainly not lend me her power to heal," I said.

Ana put her hands on mine, and showed me once again. I did it, tentatively, but she nodded that the gestures were correct.

I returned to the bedroom, not thinking, just packing. Moments later, Ana and one of her daughters appeared. I thought they had come to say good-bye. Ana walked up to me and looked me in the eye. "You are on your own," she said. "You can do it. You have been ready for a long time. You know how to do it. You are now a curandera, with my blessings."

I burst out crying. Ana burst out crying. Her daughter burst out crying. We didn't talk. We hugged and hugged and bid each other good-bye. I grabbed my belongings and left.

On December 31st, in the early afternoon, an old friend who lives in San Miguel de Allende dropped me off in Llanito. I was carrying sweaters, coats, hats, cameras, and a plastic bag full of food; I wondered how I could schlepp everything around all day and all night. I began to talk to people who arrived. Pilgrims—some of them crawling on their knees—had come to pray for healing from El Señor de los Afligidos. Hundreds of people began to descend upon the village, setting up camp in the courtyard of the church. They lit fires and cooked food. They curled up on the ground in blankets and went to sleep. It seemed odd that in the middle of such devotion and piety, there were also rides and food booths and an air of merriment in Llanito. I was offered food by the pilgrims, but declined. I accepted fresh bread that had been baked by breadmakers from a faraway village who had come on a pilgrimage. I trudged around, wondering where to park my body.

After several hours, I talked to a young taxi driver and told him my predicament. I could deposit my belongings at his grandparents' house, he told me. He took me there, introduced me to his wife and young daughter, and when he left the room for a moment, his wife grabbed my arm.

"Our marriage is so hard," she said. "My husband had a terrible childhood. He was treated worse than a dog. He turned to drugs and alcohol and it is very hard for him to stop. We have a child now. We have so little money. We live with my husband's grandparents but they are cold to him. We pay them rent, but they still treat us like unwelcome guests. If my husband would stop drinking and using drugs, I know we could make it on our own."

Without us realizing it, the taxi driver had entered the room, and when he heard what his wife was saying, he dropped his head to his chest in shame.

I felt terrible for them—they were so young and so dear—and I invited them be my guests for New Year's Eve: rides, food, whatever they wanted. They happily agreed.

Late at night, all the revelers gathered in front of the church to watch Indian dancers in gorgeous feathered attire perform the *Danza Azteca*, a centuries-old ceremonial tradition. The wife was standing next to me, and she started crying, telling me how difficult their life had been and how they had no adults who cared about them. They felt lost and they needed help.

I knew what I had to do. I had no choice. It was almost midnight. "Would you like a healing?" I asked them.

They both said, yes, yes, they really wanted a cleansing, a healing for the New Year.

And so it happened. At 11:45 P.M. on New Year's Eve, I walked to the most powerful of the calvarios, being careful to avoid the evidence of black witchcraft, lit a white candle I'd purchased in the chapel, and began to pray over the couple in Hebrew. It seemed normal to them, and oddly normal to me. I wasn't afraid. I prayed from my heart, using gestures and words Ana had taught me, but filtered though my own upbringing. In a language that didn't seem alien coming from my lips, I prayed and prayed and prayed.

My last night in Mexico, I ate dinner out and came back to the apartment where I was staying in San Miguel de Allende. As I put the key in the front door, I heard someone call my name. I turned around and saw Ana getting out of a cab. She had come all the way from Juventino Rosas. How did she know the precise moment to arrive? She looked at me. I looked at her.

"I did it, Ana," I said. "Just like you told me. I was a curandera on New Year's Eve in Llanito. I don't know if I was able to help the people, but I did my best. I tried my hardest."

She grinned, and nodded her approval.

When I came back to the United States, I struggled with whether or not I wanted to practice what I had learned from Ana in Mexico. Like Jacob in the desert, I went to sleep. I didn't lie on the ground and place a stone under my head, as he did, but, like him, I had a very intense and prophetic dream. Jacob's dream ladder reached to Heaven, and angels were climbing up and down. Mine led to a healing room, where people with problems were coming and going. The Lord offered Jacob the land and said his descendants would be as numerous as the specks of dust on the earth. My dream offered me clients who showed up morning, afternoon, evening, and night. Jacob woke up afraid and knew he was in the House of God and the place he was in was the gate to Heaven. I woke up terrified and knew that my becoming a practicing healer was the gate to a personal Hell. Jacob's place was a bridge between Heaven and earth. Mine was the bridge between a great, adventurous life and being confined and trapped. Jacob changed his name to Israel and became the father of the twelve tribes. I changed my direction and became the master of my own life.

I decided to use what I had learned from Ana only when and where it seemed appropriate, spontaneous, and right. I would never charge for it or make a profession of it, but would offer it when I thought it could help.

I used my newly-acquired skills on my husband, Paul, who had a thyroid condition. I removed negative energy from a friend who was the victim of envidia or envy at work. An acquaintance had sciatic pain, so I agreed to do what I could.

It snowballed quickly. People started asking me for healings, and their needs were sometimes serious and urgent. Working with them was depleting and draining. They called early in the morning and late at night. I was haunted by the hellish overwhelming dream. It was definitely time to stop. Ana's destiny was to be a practicing curandera. Mine was not. I would help people with whatever I knew about healing and transforming negative energy, but it would be in other, more informal ways.

Without any hesitation, I thanked Ana from the bottom of my heart, and I put my rain stick away.

Ana's path was not my path, but her impact on me was enormous.

I was raised in a specific culture with a particular religion. Although the formal practice and observances never called to me, my background provided me with an ethical, moral, and spiritual foundation and a firm connection to my ancestors . . . from a village in Ukraine all the way back to the foremothers and forefathers in the Hebrew Bible. I honored my lineage but I also longed to know more about other peoples' traditions and ways of being in the world.

My apprenticeship with Ana touched something very deep in me. Her religion and her culture are the core of her life and her healing. And yet, when it came time for me to step forward and practice the skills I had learned from her, she respected the language, religion, values, and belief system I grew up with. There was no judgment; on the contrary, there was total acceptance of the difference between us.

This was the kind of cultural exchange that propels me to set out, travel, explore, test, try on, adapt, adopt, and discover other ways of being in the world. While holding onto to my own values and beliefs, I am open to the diverse observances that exist everywhere in the world.

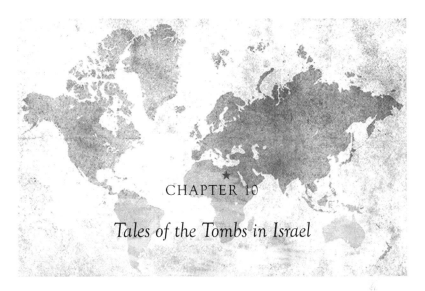

CHAPTER 10

Tales of the Tombs in Israel

I T CERTAINLY WAS ODD. An Israeli kindergarten teacher, who seemed intelligent and sane, looked me in the eyes as she explained how she met her husband. "I was forty years old, and I was just about to give up on meeting a mate. Then I prayed at the tomb of Jonathan ben Uziel, and two weeks later I met him. Eight months later we were married."

I chalked it up to coincidence until I met an Israeli artist who was bubbly, upbeat, and very credible. "My life has changed," she said. "I was so lonely but then I prayed at the tomb of Jonathan ben Uziel and met my soul mate."

I was visiting Safed, in the vicinity of the tomb, and decided to check out the departed matchmaker. Armed with a healthy dose of skepticism, I entered the women's side of the low, whitewashed building, called a *tsyun*. The tsyun is made of local rocks, cement, earth, and stones, and houses the remains of the famed first-century C.E. rabbi.

Inside, a dark velvet cloth was draped over the sepulcher. Women prayed earnestly from Hebrew prayer books and several deposited coins and bills into charity tins. The room was littered with prayer offerings: brightly-colored cloth, silk and chiffon scarves, plastic hair ornaments, and underpants. Underpants?!

I was in Israel on a personal mission. I was born and raised Jewish, but I was disaffected from institutional Judaism. Over the past few decades,

I had bathed my soul in the spiritual waters of many different traditions, but, for me, the world of synagogues and formal, standardized prayer books was dry and uninspiring. I longed for deep connection; I wanted to be stirred, moved, and transported to transcendent realms. It hadn't happened for me in America, but maybe it would happen in Israel. So even though the media assaulted us with daily images of Arabs and Jews attacking, shooting, bombing and threatening to kill each other, I was determined to find out if there was anything spiritual, mystical, healing, and holy in the Holy Land.

That is what had brought me and my husband, Paul, to the town of Safed in the area known as the Gallilee, in the north of Israel. Although he had little interest in religion, holiness, or other affairs of the spirit (he dismissively lumped all of it under the heading of superstition), Paul had agreed to photograph whatever I found.

"This is where legendary rabbis inspired the Hebrew people thousands of years ago. It is also where, in the medieval period, brilliant rabbis developed and disseminated the mystical Torah studies known as Kabbalah," our guide, Nurit, told us.

The hills around Safed are dotted with ancient tombs. To Jewish believers, these tombs of long-deceased *tsaddikim*, or holy men, are the meeting place between the living and the dead. People make pilgrimages to the burial places to ask for blessings, favors, surcease from suffering.

"They do not actually pray to the ancient rabbis; rather, they pray that the departed tsaddikim will intercede on their behalf with God," Nurit explained. "And because God looks favorably upon holy men and the merit of their lives, he is more likely to grant a request."

I wanted the hills surrounding Safed to be a spiritual place for me, but at the tomb of Rabbi Uziel, I was interested and amused, not inspired. Paul came out of the men's side (men and women are separated in Orthodox Judaism) and when I asked him what had happened, he tersely responded, "Nothing."

Nevertheless, I decided to visit one other grave in the small, ancient village of Meron—perched on the side of Mount Meron, with its abundant greenery, trees, and views of Safed and the Galilee. Meron village is the resting place of Shimon bar Yochai. One of the most famous of the tsaddikim, he is credited with being the author of the central book of Kabbalah, called the Zohar, almost two thousand years ago. Believers go to his grave to pray for prosperity, peace in their souls, fertility, and healing.

Paul and I climbed up the narrow main street of Meron to two stone archways with Hebrew inscriptions (one arch for men and one for women) that led to the whitewashed tsyun. Paul entered the men's section, looked around, shot a few photos, shrugged, and exited. "Don't ask. Nothing happened," he said pointedly. "Nothing."

But for me, things would be very different and unexpected.

As soon as I entered the women's side of the tsyun, my body started to shake and I began to sob. I looked around, self-conscious. A few women sat on benches and others stood facing the walls or the tomb itself, praying. No one was paying any attention to me as I wept, drenching the front of my pale blue shirt. I walked—no, I wove to the tomb, placed my head on the cool, white exterior, and prayed and cried for healing for my thinning bones. And I felt as though—how can I describe this?—I felt as though my words were heard.

When I came out into the stark afternoon sun, Paul was waiting for me. I had been gone about twenty minutes. I told him what had happened, and he listened. He was surprised, but couldn't really connect to it.

For hours afterwards, tears welled up in my eyes. I knew that something had happened to me at the tomb of Shimon bar Yochai, but I didn't know what it was.

Our next stop was the tomb of Baba Sali in Netivot. Baba Sali was a Moroccan holy man who is credited with many miraculous healings. He died in 1984 and has a very large following in North Africa and Israel. I was turned off as soon as I arrived at the large and well-developed site with its multiple buildings; it felt institutionalized. A well-dressed male employee spoke to visitors, droning on and on about buildings and books and the history of the place. There were glossy pamphlets and wall plaques, and I wandered off to try to find a connection, a feeling, something personal and meaningful.

Outside the tomb, a bus arrived and I watched as a line of Yemenite women got out. For some reason, I was immediately drawn to them, and I began to talk to them in English, broken Hebrew, French, and hand signals. One of them, an older woman, grabbed my hand, and I followed her. She took me to a small booth where a man sold boxes of candles. I did as she did and purchased one box for about two dollars. Then she led me to a large outdoor furnace where a fire was burning. One by one, she removed each of the twelve candles from her box. "Each one is a family member or good friend," she explained. "I pray for them." She prayed softly over each candle and tossed it into the fire. "Now you, now you," she urged.

Once again, I did as she did—asking for romance for friends, healing for a sick family member, general well-being for people I care about. Then she headed into one of the rooms, and announced, reverently, "Baba Sali." She placed her hands on a tomb and began to pray. I watched. Several of the other Yemenite women joined her and did the same thing. They prayed aloud, fervently, obviously in a state of great devotion.

A small group of tourists arrived and their guide began to speak in English about the tomb. "This is where the architect who built the Baba Sali Center is buried," the guide explained.

I felt terrible for my new Yemenite friend. She was praying at the wrong tomb! I decided to tell her this wasn't where her beloved Baba Sali was interred so that she could redirect her prayers. To my surprise, the news didn't disturb her or her friends at all.

"If this was the Baba Sali architect or someone else, it doesn't matter," said one of them.

It was a person associated with Baba Sali, and that was good enough for them. They continued to pray, and then they moved on to the actual tomb of Baba Sali and prayed once more. At each spot, they wept and intoned until it was time for them to board the bus. When my new friend hugged me good-bye, she put her hand over her heart and sighed. "Good, good," she said. It was clear that she had gotten from Baba Sali what she'd come for.

I felt as though I was on the trail of something—something vague that I couldn't articulate or define. I began to ask Israelis about other tombs.

They told me that the major annual tomb event would be taking place in a few days at the gravesite of Shimon bar Yochai, and it was important to go there before sunset.

Great. I already knew where it was. I would go back. Paul agreed without much enthusiasm—I supposed he figured it was the price he had to pay for being married to me. And so, on the holiday of Lag B'Omer, in the merry month of May, we headed to Meron.

Lag B'Omer is a spring holiday that is associated with bringing barley offerings to the ancient Temple in Jerusalem more than two millennia ago. Over the centuries, several tragic events happened at this time of year, and it is a period of semi-mourning for observant Jews. But on Lag B'Omer, there was surcease from suffering, miracles occurred, and the day is happy and celebratory.

When we arrived at Meron, the place was unrecognizable. Pilgrims had to park ten or even twenty minutes away because the roads were jammed with cars. The town's streets were bursting with women, children, and bearded men dressed in traditional Orthodox black; well over a hundred thousand believers came from all over Israel to pay homage to Shimon bar Yochai on the anniversary of his death.

"He was the most joyous of the rabbis, and on his deathbed he revealed the light of the Torah to his students. He asked that his death be marked with festivity," an Orthodox rabbi named Mendy explained to us.

It was clear that Shimon bar Yochai's devotees followed his wishes, and they arrived in a state of celebratory exuberance.

The main street was like a carnival. Vendors in makeshift booths sold crafts, religious objects, clothes, books, dates and nuts and soft drinks. Families were camped out in tents. Men in long beards asked for charity or offered blessings.

"According to tradition, if a man and woman are having fertility problems, the man gives out the contents of eighteen bottles of wine on Lag B'Omer to cure the barrenness," Rabbi Mendy informed us.

The number eighteen is favorable in Judaism, and it is associated with life and living. The origin of this belief seems to come from the two

Hebrew letters—chet and yud—that form the word "*chai*," which means life. In Gematria, or numerology, chet equals eight and yud is ten. If you add them up, you get eighteen.

Young men pressed glasses of wine on Paul and me as we walked through the street; we drank, of course, because we knew they were trying to dispense the contents of eighteen bottles and it would be rude not to honor their desire for children.

Loud Hebrew music blasted from loud speakers. On huge screens, there was a video of the much-admired Lubavitcher Rabbi, and people handed out fliers and prayer cards which bore the name of Nachman of Bratslav, another famed rabbi and mystic. People hawked wares and generally hung out. Was this Meron or a county fair?

As the sun disappeared in the west, a great bonfire was prepared near the tomb of Shimon bar Yochai.

"When Rabbi Shimon revealed the Torah on his deathbed, there was a blazing light around him, and everyone saw it," explained a woman standing next to me. "To this day, he is associated with light, and fires are lit in his honor."

It was very difficult to see what was going on because of the thousands of people gathered near the sepulcher. Paul held his camera over his head, clicking away. A rabbi poured olive oil and the bonfire blazed—marking the formal beginning of the festivities. Immediately, there was an eruption of ecstasy. Men in black began to dance and sing. Everyone clapped and stomped and hooted with glee. Men wrapped their prayer shawls and fringed undergarments around each other. They danced, they bonded, they were transported with merriment. Women danced in a circle. Everyone shared food, drinks, blessings.

By tradition, men bring their young sons to get their first haircuts on this night, so the actual tomb was mobbed. I was curious about what the faithful did inside the sepulcher, but women were not allowed entry. Paul decided to squeeze his way in so that he could get some photos. It took him about five minutes to work his way through the crowd, and I expected him to return in a minute or two, which is generally the limit of his tolerance for religious exposure.

Half an hour passed, and suddenly I saw Paul. His face was flushed. "What happened?" I asked, afraid he'd had a negative experience.

"I got pulled into the dancing," he answered. "I was going to drop out, but I figured maybe I should just go with the experience. I had no idea what I was doing. I just followed what the others did. I put my hands around the shoulders of the men next to me, and I kicked up my heels. There were dozens and dozens of men in the dance."

"Did you enjoy it?"

"Enjoy?"

"Yes. Was it fun?"

Paul grew very quiet. "It took me by surprise," he said. "It wasn't really about fun. I found it oddly bonding and moving. It was meaningful."

I looked around me. This was not the cerebral, institutionalized Judaism I had found so empty. It was an outpouring of joyful, crazy, irrational ecstasy. Whether I agreed with their brand of Orthodox Judaism or not, it was undeniable that these men in black and their families were moved and transported and had faith.

Faith. Yes. That was the key to it all. It was faith that made women looking for their soul mates leave behind scarves and underpants at the tomb of Rabbi Uziel. It was faith that I felt when I entered the sepulchral building that housed Shimon bar Yochai. Faith that I could be healed. Over the years, millions of people had entered that same room, praying for favors and for healing; they had left behind a palpable energy that had emanated from their prayers and tears. It was faith that brought the Yemenite women to the tomb of Baba Sali, faith that he and everyone associated with him would help them to find well-being. And it was faith in the streets of Meron on Lag B'Omer. The belief that young couples could become fertile, that the spirit of Rabbi Shimon was hovering around, that humans could be blessed with prosperity and community and wholeness. That through the year-round study of torah and mysticism, they could find union with humankind and with God.

When I came home, I started to notice people all around me who yearned to be moved in their souls. Some of them were transported by music. Others by nature or art, cooking or ministering to their elders.

I felt a longing to be connected to the dead, to transcend the bound-aries of time and space. I bought a Yahrzeit candle, which is the com-memorative candle-in-a-glass that Jewish people light every year on the anniversary of the death of their near and dear ones. After dinner, when the phones weren't ringing and my computer was in sleep mode, I lit the candle and began to talk to my father, Eddie, who died when I was young. His passing left a deep, unfillable hole. Not only had he been deprived of a full life, but I had spent all of my adult existence without a father.

First I told him what was going on in my life. I spoke about my work, my marriage to Paul, how my mother was doing. I said I had been to Israel where I visited the tombs of the rabbis. I talked freely about this and that, and then I began to ask him questions. "Are you okay?" "Are you at peace?" "Are you watching over us?" "Do you think I am doing the right thing with my life?"

All of the questions could be answered by "yes" or "no." And I swear to you that when the answer was "yes," the flame of the candle grew bigger. And when the reply was "no," the flame flitted horizontally from side to side.

Was I imagining it? I don't think so. Is it really that easy for the living to access the deceased? If both parties are willing, I believe the answer is "yes."

Maybe I just have faith or a yearning in my soul to connect to some-thing larger than me. If you have faith, you may want to try it.

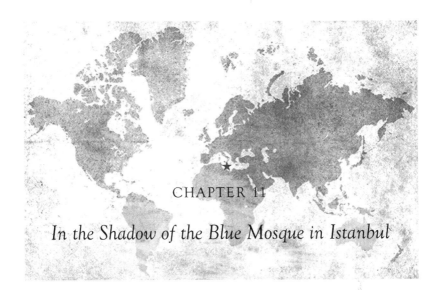

CHAPTER 11

In the Shadow of the Blue Mosque in Istanbul

ISTANBUL, TURKEY, probably has as many great hotels as it has kabob skewers, but a small, clean, simple hotel called the Zeynap Sultan is one of the top-rated places to stay in the city.

It's in the historic Sultanahmet area of Istanbul, where it shares space with the nearby Blue Mosque (an early seventeenth-century marvel adorned with blue tiles); the domes and minarets of the sixth-century architectural masterpiece Aya Sophia; the Byzantine hippodrome where chariot races once took place; the archeology museum; Topkapi Palace; restaurants and shops which offer everything from silk carpets to caftans worn by a harem beauty, to silver-threaded towels and shawls from an Ottoman bride's trousseau, to baseball caps and T-shirts.

Breakfast is served on the roof of the hotel, and guests absent-mindedly eat yoghurt, olives, cheese, and hard-boiled eggs as they look out over some of the most beloved tourist sites in the world. And this is where most guests meet Abe Akyunus, the owner of the hotel. "It was once my family home," he tells them.

Something must be wrong with Abe. Although he once owned and ran a pharmacy and developed cutting-edge products for the cosmetic and beauty industry, he never learned that business is about money. He's so clueless about the bottom line that he drops everything and shuttles guests around, makes calls for them, and folds himself in half and in half again, like the hotel's sheets, to make his clients happy.

83

If you spend any time talking to Abe, he'll probably invite you into the bowels of the hotel, which used to be the basement of his childhood home. He'll hand you a flashlight and lead you down rickety steps to what may be among the oldest examples of Byzantine architecture in the city. You'll see remnants of frescos and pillars that were possibly part of an early church—maybe even older than Aya Sofia.

Abe was born Muslim, but he is horrified by organized religion. Probably the only thing he won't do for you is pull out a Koran, accompany you to a religious service, or engage in serious conversation about Sufis, whirling dervishes, mysticism, prayer, prophets, or phylacteries. He is an equal opportunity secularist; no organized religion is more or less attractive or interesting to him.

Some guests only know Abe as the friendly hotel guy who waves and asks how their day was and what they did. They notice that he really listens and, if they express any need, he tries to fulfill it. Others have tea with Abe and he regales them with funny, sad, and crazy stories of growing up in the fabled city. A few experience "essential Abe" if they get sick and he checks in on them or if they say they have heard about the fabulous dried fruits at the Egyptian spice market and suddenly they're being proffered apricots or figs.

"Hey, Abe, you're a middle-aged guy. You're working insane hours. You have more than enough money. Don't you ever get tired of ministering to your clients?" I ask.

He looks at me as though I need a lobotomy. "They are guests in my house," he says. "Do you expect me to ignore them?"

I have become very close to Abe and his wife, Gulhis, over the years. I was a guest at his hotel, stayed in their house, and once Abe drove seventeen hours to take me from Bodrum (which was Halicarnassus in ancient times and produced homeboy historian Herodotus) to Istanbul. We speak on the phone regularly, exchange emails, and have spent long hours together. I have never seen Abe be anything other than generous and hospitable. Even after the seventeen-hour drive, when his eyes looked like glazed donuts, he wanted to be sure I had a good dinner and was comfortable for the night.

Abe's hotel is all about Abe. And when Abe's not there, his staff has been trained to treat guests the way he does: with care, concern, and boundless hospitality. No wonder the place beats out so many other hotels that offer startling architecture, sumptuous rooms, and five-star amenities.

Abe enjoys creature comforts, luxury, ease, and the finer things in life. But the very finest thing to him is human relationships and helping others. He does not believe we were born to shop, consume, and then die. He feels good when he makes others feel comfortable and respected. He gets high when he helps his friends. Despite his secularism, Abe has penetrated the core of what religions are about: doing to others as you would have them do to you and practicing care, concern, and what my Buddhist friends call lovingkindness.

In a world of bottom lines and spreadsheets, this one man reminds us that a business can do well by doing good things for people. In a sense, you *can* take good will to the bank because people are drawn to establishments where they feel nurtured and cared for. They will frequent them again and again and tell all their friends. It all boils down to one word: service. In dreamy Istanbul, this is the secret of Abe's success.

CHAPTER 12

Happy Among the Hmong or at Home: Zen Travel

I WAS UNCHARACTERISTICALLY AND DEEPLY UNHAPPY. Maybe it was the bitter cold, or the overwork, stress, insomnia, and exhaustion. I had surfed the Internet and rented a little cottage half a block from the beach in San Diego. My fantasy was waking up to pale golden light streaming in through the windows, saluting the sun, languorously stretching on an exercise mat unfurled on the polished pine floor. After a light, healthy breakfast in an outdoor café, there would be a walk along the ocean, watching surfers and communing with the waves. In the afternoon, a rented paddle boat would glide gently through the water. As the sun retired for the day, it would linger for a moment in the backyard where I sipped margaritas, watching the pink and gold afterglow that illuminated the heavens.

Reality intruded. It was winter and San Diego was groaning under the lashing of storms, cold, ill winds, and torrential rains. The little dream cottage was a nightmare of dog dander, dust, dirt, half-eaten blobs of food in the fridge, illegal and hazardous wiring, lack of insulation, and a tiny heater the size of two fists. If we plugged in a hairdryer, the fuse blew. As I sat in darkness, Paul crawled through the only closet—past the dust and hangers draped with the homeowner's suits, wetsuits, T-shirts, shorts, and pants; past his salted-away hardcore magazines with photos of engorged parts and lip-licking ladies; past the single, plastic shoe rack that was allotted to us for our clothes—and groped around to reconnect the loose wires that hung off the wall.

To make matters worse, there was nowhere to drive. The streets were blocked off because of flooding, and cars were half-submerged in water laced with huge, dirty palm fronds. We sat inside, huddled around the minuscule heater, trying to crank up the physical and psychic energy to disengage from our contract, find another place to rent, and, if all else failed, drag our weary carcasses onto a plane headed for somewhere warm . . . like sub-Saharan Africa.

When the streets finally cleared, all we could think of was shopping for fleece, fluffy, warm bathrobes, and industrial sprays to mask dog smell. We were devoid of energy, imagination, and life force.

We couldn't believe this had happened to us. Normally, you could drop us in the middle of the desert and we'd realize the fascination of sand. Once, at a resort, when we were awakened in the middle of the night because flames were leaping toward our cabin and we had to leave behind all our belongings and run to safety, we turned disaster into discovery as we spent hours interviewing the other survivors. But there we were in spectacular coastal California, bummed out, burned out, shivering and, for the first time in our travel lives, bored. The dismal little cottage had a huge TV, and we torpidly watched actors, athletes, and advertisers prance, parade, run, walk, slither, leap, sell, fall in love, and jockey for power on the screen.

One day the skies cleared, the sun emerged, and we were sitting in a restaurant, sinking our forks into breakfast burritos the size of our thighs. I was perusing a throwaway paper that I had picked up at a rack near the entry door, when I saw a small notice about Hmong New Year in a nearby public park in Kearney Mesa. I began to feel a stirring, a frisson of interest and curiosity.

I had known about the Hmong (pronounced "Mong") mountain people for decades. In the sixties, the U.S. recruited ethnic Hmong soldiers to fight on our side in the Vietnam War and help us conduct a protracted secret war in Laos. This resulted, of course, in thousands of deaths and casualties and, when the war was over, there were terrible reprisals in Laos against the Hmong. Many fled to refugee camps in Thailand and the U.S. promised to resettle them, but the process has been difficult, controversial, wrought with duplicity, and painfully slow. Today, there are almost a quarter of a million Hmong in the U.S.

I asked a few people I knew in San Diego if they wanted to go with us to the exotic New Year celebration. They declined, adding that the Hmong aren't friendly and it was probably a small, immigrant event that wouldn't be of much interest.

We went anyway. The section of the park reserved for the festivities was ablaze with the dazzling traditional clothing of the hundreds of Hmong who came from all over the country for the celebration. Paul and I were the only non-Hmong there. I didn't know what to explore first: booths with native food and drink; stands laden with intricate embroidery, accessories, and clothes for sale; a lion dance; or a potluck with huge casseroles of food prepared and offered for free by Hmong women.

I was juggling a platter of pickled and spicy vegetables, green papaya salad, sausage, chicken, and a sweet drink with tapioca when something caught my eye: a row of teenage or twenty-something Hmong men gently throwing tennis balls to a row of young women of about the same age. I watched until my food started to get cold, and then I wandered over to a wooden table to eat. As I was savoring the little-known Southeast Asian delicacies, I looked up and saw another row of boys tossing tennis balls to a line of girls opposite them.

"Excuse me," I said to a middle-aged couple at my table. "Can you tell me what that game is?"

"It's how our young people meet each other," the man said.

"They come from Wisconsin, Sacramento, everywhere to maybe find a Hmong husband or wife," the woman added, grinning.

Other Hmong joined in the conversation.

"While they throw the ball back and forth, they talk," said a stunning woman decked out in a long black dress trimmed with red embroidery. "Maybe a girl asks how old a boy is or they exchange names. If they find out the other person is from the same family, it's not a suitable partner."

89

"Is there ever love at first throw?" I asked.

"Oh yes," said my beautiful interlocutor, laughing. "And if a boy likes a girl, he will begin to sing to tell her about her wonderful qualities."

"He literally sings?" I asked.

The woman nodded. "Singing to express love is very important in our culture."

I walked over to the lines of potential mates, trying to guess where the tennis balls might lead to a match ending in love, musing that if I were single I would much prefer casually tossing words and tennis balls to hooking up with someone in a bar or fidgeting at a singles' event. I would have happily stood there watching for hours, but my attention was drawn by a crowd gathered in front of a booth that sold CDs and DVDs. The man who ran the booth slipped a documentary film into a DVD player.

On a small screen, a young Hmong girl in the mountains of Laos was singing and sobbing. Opposite her, an older man looked on with compassion. The girl's voice was hypnotic and the sounds seemed to come from her soul.

I inquired of a man standing next to me, "Could you tell me, please, what the girl is saying?"

The man turned his face to me, and I could see that he was crying too. Tears pooled in his big, brown eyes and then trickled down his chin onto his neatly-pressed white shirt. He seemed to have no embarrassment about weeping in front of a stranger.

"She is an orphan and she is telling the story of how she has suffered. She is alone in the world. Her family is dead and she has no one. That man says he wants to help her. He is too old to marry her, but she can come and stay at his house for as long as she wants."

"But why is she singing?" I asked.

"In our culture, we sing our sorrows," he answered. He wiped his tears with his hand and added, "I am crying because her story is my story too. I am also an orphan. I had nobody to help me. I suffered the way she is suffering. I endured what she had to endure."

"I am so sorry," I muttered. "Thank you for telling me. Thank you for teaching me."

The man handed me his card. "If you go to visit the Hmong people in Laos, I can accompany you and show you around. I will introduce you to our people. I am so happy you came here to share our New Year with us."

It was a sentiment that was repeated. All day, Hmong people kept thanking me for coming and for being interested in their culture.

Of course I was interested! In one day, I had gotten to learn about people who sing their sorrows and joys, take pride in their national dress, and find love in a simple, sweet ball game. I had sampled Southeast Asian cuisine I knew nothing about, heard the Hmong language, experienced the power of a man weeping in public, listened to music I didn't know, bought an embroidered and tasseled indigenous hat. And I didn't have to crank up enormous energy, buy a plane ticket, plan an itinerary, or spend much money. All I had to do was drive for twenty minutes to soak up a bit of faraway Laos in San Diego.

For days, I had been mired in depression, disengagement, and listlessness. How extraordinary that one state of being had so rapidly morphed into another. I marveled at how other cultures drew me out of myself, into a world that was larger and infinitely more interesting than the malaise inside of me. I was filled with admiration for the Hmong, who had overcome such adversity. I was grateful that, once again, I was excited by learning, by contact with people whose life experiences and culture were so different from my own.

When Paul and I returned to the creepy cottage that evening, we rediscovered our mojo. We simply refused to be unhappy. We moved to a charming place where we could sleep soundly, put our clothes in drawers, turn on a wall heater, and walk along the Strand in Pacific Beach, and Sunset Cliffs in Ocean Beach; a place where we could appreciate the seemingly effortless grace of surfers, sip margaritas, smile at the sun and feel grateful for every droplet of our lives.

Travel is a balm for my soul, but I don't always need to go far to experience it. When we returned home, I tuned into the different ethnicities and customs all around me. Paul and I went to an Aztec ceremony at El Museo Cultural De Santa Fe, where gloriously-attired dancers honored Cuahtemoc, whom they call the first defender of the Americas, and celebrated what they described as the first direction for Nuestro Señor del Sacremontes. The drumming was loud and exciting, and the dancers, many with rattles around their ankles, leapt, twirled, and stepped with intention and devotion. During a break in the dancing, we stood silently in front of an altar contemplating the tall white candles and the offerings of flowers, musical instruments, photos, and food.

On Chinese New Year, we dined at a local restaurant where there were four dancing lions—including a huge black one. We stuffed money into red envelopes and plunged them into a lion's mouth to ensure prosperity and good fortune. And we ate Middle Eastern food while we watched the sinuous stomach muscles of belly dancers.

Finding these events was easy. All I had to do was look at bulletin boards, magazines, newspapers, and websites. With minimal expense of effort, I was rewarded with new connections, instant learning, expansion of my horizons, and a richer, more textured and deliciously varied life.

Travel is a Zen activity that can lift me out of my inner life into engagement with the world around me. There is so much happening—new people, ideas, food, customs, language, sounds, smells—that it literally yanks me from inward to outward focus. No longer trekking through the muck of the past or anticipating an uncertain future, I am plunked right into the present, where healing, happiness, and renewal take place.

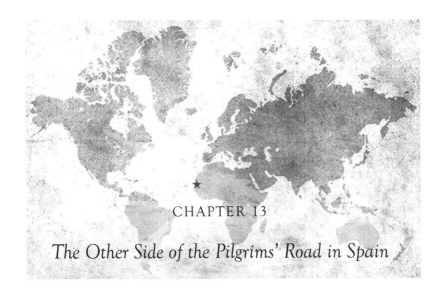

CHAPTER 13

The Other Side of the Pilgrims' Road in Spain

ROM THE FIRST TIME I HEARD ABOUT IT, I had a burning desire to go. I wanted to be a pilgrim, stripped down to whatever I could carry on my back, trekking five hundred miles from St. Jean-Pied-de-Port in southern France to the final destination of the Cathedral of Santiago de Compostela in northwestern Spain, which purportedly contains the tomb of St. James. I pictured myself turning inward, timing my footsteps to my breath, meditating, unplugged from news, my computer, phone, fax and, most of all, social chitchat. Inane conversation about weather, whether or not to buy this or that, rehashing of TV shows, and minute dissections of who said what to whom grind my soul to ash. I wanted the simplicity of the medieval pilgrims who walked the Camino de Santiago de Compostela (a collection of pilgrimage routes also known as the Way of St. James). I yearned for a month-long spiritual undertaking, over hill and dale, pasture and plain, carrying the iconic scallop shell which signifies to others that you are, quite literally, walking the walk.

Twenty-five years ago, a few thousand devoted pilgrims followed the Way of St. James every year; today estimates are in the 100,000 to 200,000 range. The pilgrims come on foot, bike, and horseback. A few even bring donkeys. Some do the whole walk and others complete a section, hopping on a train or bus for part of the pilgrimage. They are young and old, fit and unfit, short, tall, fat, thin, bearded, shaven, rich, poor, educated, unschooled, religious, non-believers and the just plain curious. They are easy to spot; they carry walking sticks and huge backpacks. A few months ago, I set my feet on the Camino for the first time.

At a public hostel for pilgrims, I met a buoyant young man from London who was standing patiently in line, waiting to get his pilgrim's credential booklet stamped. When he got to Santiago, the stamps would serve as proof that he had walked the Camino, or at least the last sixty-two miles of it, and this would qualify him for a pilgrim's certificate.

"How far did you walk today?" I asked him.

"About twenty-five miles," he replied.

"May I lift your backpack to see how heavy it is?"

"Sure," he answered, with the good humor that was characteristic of most pilgrims I met.

I bent over and raised it up; more accurately, I *tried* to lift it. It weighed more than fifty pounds. The young man was grinning and I was mortified. My back ached before I had taken one step on the Camino. What was I thinking? I hated carrying anything. Some days, my handbag was too much for me. I loved being unencumbered, physically free.

I peered inside the hostel; beds were lined up in a gymnasium-sized room. Each had a blanket, but no sheets. There was zero privacy. A gaggle of walkers waited to take cold showers because there was no hot water. In a small courtyard next to the hostel, people were soaking their blisters and icing their tendonitis-inflamed legs. One pallid woman said she was so exhausted she didn't know if she could go on the next day. It was then I knew that I would never be a pilgrim. It was fine for others. But for me it was a fantasy. A dream. A demented delusion.

Why, I wondered, did anyone walk the Camino? I began to ask the pilgrims I met. In a municipal pilgrims' *albergue*, or hostel, three young men were cooking eggs for dinner in the small kitchen area. They devoured them with mounds of tortellini and cheese sauce. One of them said he was walking the Camino before he started engineering school. A second had been laid off and decided to make a pilgrimage before going back to work.

"I'm not sure why I'm doing it," said the third. "But I can tell you that the socializing at night is the best part. You drink beer or wine and you meet people. The three of us didn't know each other before."

I stopped at a private albergue, which offered separate rooms with baths for pilgrims who wanted more comfort.

"I just went through a divorce," said a middle-aged woman, sitting in a lounge chair nursing a beer. "It's very meaningful for me to be here, with no contact from my ex, away from my familiar surroundings, thinking about who I am besides a wife."

Ahh, I said to myself, *maybe if I stayed at a place like this, I could bear the walk.* Whom was I kidding? I learned that last year there was a plague of bedbugs in both the municipal and private hostels. And some of the private albergues were as basic as the public ones.

In Rabanal, I met Abraham from the Canary Islands, Francisco from Tenerife, and José Luis from Salamanca. The three new friends sat under a tree nursing their tired feet. For them, the Camino was an inexpensive vacation; they could explore a region of Spain they didn't know, and it would give them a sense of accomplishment to finish it.

A Korean woman said she had learned about the Camino on television, and then she read an inspiring book by a Korean writer about the pilgrimage walk. It sealed the deal.

Alexander from Vienna quit his job as a banker because it didn't suit him. He was walking to ponder what he would do next.

"I'm not talking to other pilgrims about it," he said. "It's more about me and my own thoughts. I'm an athlete and I don't find the walk hard or tiring."

Two young Spanish girls said, "We walk by day and we ice at night. Our objective is to get to Santiago. We don't know why we are doing it, but we're really happy."

Judy Magee from Toronto was nervous about hauling her backpack. "Mom, don't worry about the weight of your backpack," her daughter Kaitlin had counseled her. "It weighs less than the to-do list you make every day." Judy said, "That thought is with me all the time. I'm learning to let go, and not to plan for every contingency."

Kellie, from Wales, said with a laugh that quite a few happily married couples met while walking the Camino. She wasn't exactly looking for a mate, but she wasn't ruling it out either.

The more pilgrims I spoke to, the more diverse reasons I heard for doing the walk. Some wanted fresh air and an active, outdoorsy experience. Others were intrigued by the churches and art and great Spanish food along the way. The varied landscape drew some, and the challenge called to others. There were devout Catholics, atheists, Jews, Bahai's and Buddhists. For some, it was a spiritual quest, a long prayer of gratitude, a meaningful way to mark a life transition. And more than a few were repeat pilgrims; they had done the Camino once or several times before.

I began to feel the discomfort of the outsider. They were all walking and I was watching. They were making sacrifices, and I was sleeping in hotels, driving in a car, and dining on regional foods that burst on my joyous palate.

"Maybe I'm helping the pilgrims by writing about them," I joked to one woman, and she nodded and said, quite seriously, that there is a whole tradition of people serving the Camino.

What does that mean? How do you serve a route? I wondered. So off I went, to find out about non-walking pilgrims who are somehow engaged in service to people, a path, or something else I didn't understand.

On the outskirts of Sahagún, I met loquacious, vivacious, eighty-two-year-old Paca Luna Tovar at the Virgen del Puente hermitage. Every day, Paca walks over a mile from town to the hermitage and adorns the altar with flowers and candles that are dedicated to the Virgin. She carries with her *galletas de hierro* (a regional cookie) and fiery, alcoholic aguardiente for the pilgrims who come inside. While I was there, she spontaneously broke into song; the lyrics were about the patron saint of the town, the Camino, the hermitage, and two local churches.

"My ancestors welcomed the pilgrims here," she said proudly. "When my aunts were alive, they brought me here to greet the pilgrims, and when they died, I took over. I am the fourth generation. I come to be with the pilgrims. No matter what language they speak, I understand them all, although I am not sure how this happens. The government is planning to do restoration at the hermitage, but even during the work, I will walk here every day to meet the pilgrims. If I stop my daily walk to the hermitage, it will be the end of me."

Little do the pilgrims suspect that when they drop by the hermitage and munch on cookies or accept a shot of firewater, they are helping to keep an octogenarian dynamo alive.

At a hostel in Rabanal del Camino, which is run by the Confraternity of St. James in Britain, I met Martin Singleton, who had come from London to volunteer as a *hospitalero* for two and a half weeks. He was probably in his late sixties to mid seventies, and his jobs included making breakfast and keeping the rooms clean.

Singleton's relationship with the Camino began after his wife completed a pilgrimage. "I had never walked farther than my house to the car," he said, "but I put my boots on, got an old rucksack, and went back with my wife the next year and walked 120 miles. I had no physical problems walking. It affected me spiritually. It changed me. I made a promise to come back and complete the entire Camino. I did it last year."

He confided that the second walk was less moving than the first—an experience he says many returning pilgrims share.

"It only happens once in your life," he said in a low voice. "After that, my wife and I wanted to give something back to the pilgrims, to help them along on their journey. We joined the Confraternity of St. James in England and went to meetings. We decided to become hospitaleros and here we are."

After a pause, he added, "I never did service before in my life. It's wonderful. It's a bit like the first experience I had."

In rural Moratinos, population eighteen, a former American journalist named Rebekah Scott lives with her English husband, Paddy, in an old, painstakingly restored and repaired farmhouse they call the Peaceable Kingdom. The Camino goes through the village and passes by their house, and Rebekah spoke with knowledge and enthusiasm about the famous road.

"Do you know that the churches and monumental buildings along the way are meant to be seen on horseback? The best vantage point is from four feet off the ground, where the rich could see them," she said.

Tomas, the Croatian handy man who was helping the couple, is also attached to the Camino and to a dog named Mimi he found while walking. He tried to take her with him, carried her for about twenty miles, and then was forced to leave her behind. After he reached Santiago, he went back to visit Mimi, earned a little money doing handiwork, and walked the Camino again. And again. And again.

"There is counseling for people who keep doing the walk. What will they do after they stop walking? There's a kind of post-Camino stress syndrome," Rebekah explained. "Maybe they have no work and no purpose. They can stay cheaply while they walk and depend on the generosity of strangers. They are drifters on the Camino. And then there's the whole subject of who is a pilgrim. If you stay at *paradores* (expensive hotels), are you a pilgrim? Are you one if you bike or ride a horse? In the past, people were sentenced to walk the Camino, to get them out of town. There's a whole history of people telling war stories about their walks."

Rebekah paused, served me some delicious Thai curry, and then resumed.

"When you walk, you become aware of everything; you hear the stream, the birds, your senses become acute. You lose weight, get fit. I'm a hospitalera now. I volunteer at hostels, listening to the pilgrims, cleaning up, cooking, applying first aid. It's a nice break from the ordinary. And you get to know another town."

The casual way Rebekah spoke belies her deep dedication and service to the Way of St. James. She and Paddy built a labyrinth for the pilgrims and leave small gifts there. In their barn, they have made space for the pilgrims' donkeys, horses or bikes. And in their house, they have three bedrooms for pilgrims and a bathroom where walkers can luxuriate in a tub. Rebekah also cooks for them. In her spare time, she trains hospitaleros.

Elyn Aviva recently moved from the U.S. to Sahagún, to be on the Camino. She has published fiction and nonfiction books about the holy trek; the latter deal with her walk of gratitude after cancer surgery, and her first walk, in 1982, before the Camino became so popular. She tried to explain to me her fascination, which she said borders on obsession.

"I guess I'm attracted to the Camino the way a moth is to a flame. When I first learned about it in 1981, it grabbed me by the back of my neck and it's never let me go. At various times I've thought I was 'done' with the Camino, but I keep going back to explore it from yet another angle, to write yet another book. I'm currently working on synthesizing a number of Spanish books on the esoteric, hidden symbolism of the Camino so that this information will be available in English," she said.

When I asked why she wanted to live on the road, she answered without hesitation, "It's good to be 'on the Camino' but not walking it—seeing and hearing the daily flow of pilgrims passing through, offering assistance to those in need (looking for a guidebook, needing to go to the doctor, needing someone to translate at the pharmacy or in a restaurant)—being part of the Camino while staying at home. For now."

She talked about people who served the Camino and helped her on her first walk. "They opened up a deserted schoolroom for us, or gave us food when we had none and there were no grocery stores available. I remember people running after us to point out the correct path, or calling out that we had taken the wrong route. I remember others offering to buy us drinks, or giving us something to eat. And I remember being asked to light a candle on their behalf in Santiago. Decent people, faith-filled people, ordinary people—not paid to be of service, not hired to do a job, but acting from their soul's desire, from their deep, abiding faith."

Once again, I tried to understand what it meant to serve the Camino. "So it's about serving pilgrims, rather than the road itself?" I asked.

"You could say I serve the Divine, the Great Mystery," Aviva replied with a smile.

The rest of my time in Spain, I contemplated pilgrimages and service. I visited other pilgrimage sites—like the famous fourteenth-century Monastery of Guadalupe in the picturesque town of the same name, in the Extremadura region. There, too, I saw pilgrims with enormous, weighty backpacks, sacrificing their comfort, enduring hardship and stress, pushing their limits for a higher or more important personal goal. I had already decided I was not going to walk the walk, but maybe honoring the sites was an indirect way to be of service. I had no backpack, but I had expended effort to get there: booking air travel, securing accommodations, renting a car, paying money, standing in line.

I wondered how else I could have a pilgrim experience.

Recently, I sent money to help victims of a natural disaster but I didn't actually go there to volunteer. Did my check count as service, or was it too easy to just sign my name, rip it out of my checkbook, and mail it? What about people who were even less pilgrimage prone than I was because of lack of time, stamina, desire, or money? Could they ever know the satisfaction, pride, sense of accomplishment, and service of a pilgrim? Could I?

I decided that the answer for me was no, but then, sitting in a restaurant in Trujillo, the town that spawned Pizarro, who conquered and pillaged Peru, I had a breakthrough. I had recently spent a lot of time listening and talking to a young woman who was overwhelmed by motherhood and I introduced her to another woman who was going through the same thing. They spontaneously formed a two-person support team. Before that, I had assisted a young man who was applying to college by writing him a letter of recommendation. And I called, wrote and spent time with local and faraway friends who were sick or grieving the loss of a parent, spouse, or pet. Sometimes I just listened, and other times I tried to offer help or consolation.

Maybe the new mother, the man setting out for college, and my aching friends were pilgrims, on the road of life. Perhaps helping them in some small way could be counted as giving them assistance on their path.

By the time I was sipping regional wines in a café outside of the walls of the medieval city of Cáceres, I reflected that I, too, am a pilgrim in life. And I can thank people who help me on my pilgrim's path.

When I returned home, I told a friend that I felt as though I were on a pilgrimage in life, and she was assisting me.

"What!?" she said, incredulous. "I'm not doing anything. I'm just walking and talking with you."

"And that's exactly what I need," I answered truthfully.

I said the same thing to another friend, who is struggling with a serious and, for now, incapacitating illness.

"Me? Helping you on your pilgrimage?" she asked. Then she burst out laughing. "I spend my life praying and thanking God for keeping me alive. I used to be so active. Now I feel useless—as though I have nothing to give."

I let her know that her gratitude and her faith were inspirational to me and I felt that in bearing so much discomfort she was somehow serving humanity and the universe. She twisted her mouth into a wry grin, obviously not believing me.

I told her that the most eloquent expression of the service provided by simply enduring was found in the work of the brilliant seventeenth-century English poet John Milton. The light of his life dimmed, externally, when he became blind. But his inner light shone radiantly through his poem "On His Blindness."

> When I consider how my light is spent
> E're half my days in this dark world and wide,
> And that one Talent which is death to hide,
> Lodg'd with me useless, though my Soul more bent
> To serve therewith my Maker, and present
> My true account, least he returning chide,
> Doth God exact day-labour, light deny'd,
> I fondly ask; But patience to prevent
> That murmur, soon replies, God doth not need
> Either man's work or his own gifts, who best
> Bear his milde yoke, they serve him best. His State
> Is Kingly. Thousands at his bidding speed
> And post o're Land and Ocean without rest:
> They also serve who only stand and waite.[1]

My friend grew silent and thoughtful. "I guess he was serving humanity by writing that poem," she said quietly. "People who feel discouraged and hopeless in life can still turn to him, even though he's been dead for centuries."

After a long pause, she added, "Even after death, I guess it's possible to lighten the load of life's pilgrims."

---

[1] Arthur Quiller-Couch, ed. 1919. *The Oxford Book of English Verse: 1250–1900.*

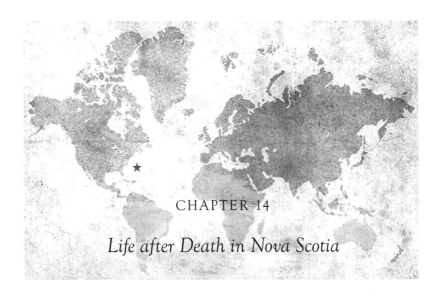

CHAPTER 14

Life after Death in Nova Scotia

A FEW YEARS AGO, I was among the tourists in St. Martinville, Louisiana, the birthplace of Cajun culture. I remember staring at the statue of Evangeline and wondering who the Cajuns were and where they came from. Their lilting, drawling French was charming, their music and dancing upbeat, and their crawfish, roux, boudin, and hearty gumbo were addictive.

I soon learned that the word "Cajun" derived from "Acadian" and that the Louisiana Cajuns were descended from Acadians who were ejected from Nova Scotia in a deportation which is sometimes referred to as a diaspora. Henry Wordsworth Longfellow had memorialized the dreadful dispersion of the Acadians in his poem, "Evangeline."

Although the heroine, Evangeline, was a fictional creation, the poem was about a very real tragedy that befell the Acadians in 1755, and Longfellow's poem, published almost a century after the events, tugged at the hearts of millions of sympathetic readers around the world who knew nothing of the horrific Acadian story.

Recently, I was in Nova Scotia, at a very moving site called Grand-Pré, and the pieces of the Acadians' story began to fall into place.

Originally from France, the Acadians had arrived in Nova Scotia, developed a sophisticated irrigation system, turned salt marshes into fertile meadows, farmed, and transformed the land into a rich breadbasket.

The most famous of their settlements was Grand-Pré. When Britain and France declared war, even though they had no reason to distrust the Acadians, the British confiscated their farmlands and livestock and forcibly herded the Acadians onto dangerously overcrowded ships which sailed off in perilous waters to unknown destinations.

In the chaos of the embarkation, grief-stricken families were torn apart. Children were separated from parents, husbands from wives, and lovers wailed as the ocean stretched out between them. The Acadians were shipped to New England, France, England, and some made their way to Louisiana. Over the course of eight years, as many as ten thousand Acadians from Grand-Pré and other villages were dispersed. More than fifty percent of them died from hunger, illness, anguish, shipwreck, forced labor, and miserable living conditions. And for many years the Acadians wandered from place to place, facing expulsions, further deportations, and the trauma of perpetual dislocation.

Today, Grand-Pré is a tourist attraction in the scenic Annapolis Valley in Nova Scotia. The visitor reception and interpretation center offers a moving and informative film about the Acadians; glass cases contain artifacts found at the site; there are archeological digs and the foundations of an Acadian dwelling, a well, a statue of Evangeline, and a cross that marks the site of the original cemetery.

To me, the highlight of the site is the memorial church which dates back to 1922. It was designed, built by, and belongs to the Acadian people. And it is the place where they have told and continue to tell their own story.

It is a commemorative, rather than a consecrated, church; it stands near the site of the original Catholic Church where the Acadian men were first rounded up in 1755 and informed that they were going to be expelled from their homeland.

Like the handful of other visitors to the church, I grew silent and contemplative as soon as I entered. On the walls were paintings of Acadian farmers in their fields, the British requiring an oath of allegiance from the Acadians who refused to give it, the reading of the Deportation Order in the church on September 5, 1775.

A stained glass window, in somber blues and grays, depicts the fateful embarkation. A rowboat overflowing with people suggests the chaos and overcrowding, and the portrayal of deportees saying goodbye to their families on shore evokes the misery of separation and loss. A red ribbon runs through the window; it represents the British color and also the tie of family. On September 5 every year, the sun shines through the window and the red line is reflected in a commemorative plaque on the opposite wall that describes the Deportation Order on that day.

But there is another element in the window that is the very heart of the Grand-Pré experience: the survival of the Acadian people is celebrated by a sunrise and the whole window is encircled in gold.

Today, there are more than three million descendants of the expulsed Acadian farmers. Some of them returned to their ancestral land in Nova Scotia, but others are spread across the Atlantic provinces of Canada, New England, France, the Falkland Islands, Belize, Haiti and, of course, Louisiana. Even though the British tried to get them to assimilate into the Anglo world, wherever they landed, they managed to retain their very vibrant and proud culture. There has actually been an Acadian renaissance. No longer satisfied to let Longfellow—who was not Acadian—be their spokesman, the Acadians are committed to telling their own story. They are reclaiming their past and shaping their present and future. Think of the Cajuns—their music, dancing, their food. They are making their mark in the world.

A young woman named Amy, an employee of Parks Canada who guards and disseminates information in the church at Grand-Pré, told me, "I was raised in this area, but I started to get 'new glasses' and understood so much more when I began working here."

What she meant was that the English version or the whitewashed story told by non-Acadians became eclipsed by the story of the Deportation from the Acadian point of view.

The day I was at Grand-Pré, I connected with Sally Ross, who wrote a book called *The Acadians of Nova Scotia*. She told me that one of the reasons so much is known about Grand-Pré is that two of the occupying

British officers kept diaries where they recorded the events of the dispersion. The diaries validate the Acadians' accounts of the atrocities.

Several years ago, the Queen of England issued a recognition of the wrong committed to the Acadians at the time of the Deportation. Not an apology, but a recognition of the Acadian version of the events.

Sally Ross told me that Grand-Pré has become a pilgrimage place for visitors and for Acadians whose ancestors lived and were buried there. That is certainly understandable, but I was surprised to also hear that Grand-Pré is considered a romantic destination. People—not necessarily Acadians—go there to propose marriage, get engaged, renew wedding vows. I saw a young couple bring their newborn baby to Grand-Pré. And I learned that older visitors to Nova Scotia insist on coming to the site for inspiration.

As I walked around the area, I couldn't get this aspect of Grand-Pré off my mind. I stood in a green field and looked at a bronze statue that depicted a wandering Acadian family: a mother, father, son, and daughter; the father held a pilgrim's staff. Why didn't the artist depict a miserable, downtrodden family? Why did they look noble, proud, strong? Why did the artist, like visitors to Grand-Pré, consider the site so uplifting? I kept thinking about this and it wasn't until after I got home that I began to assimilate what I had seen and heard.

The romantic aspect of Grand-Pré is probably easiest to understand. Longfellow's poem tells a wrenching, tragic love story of separation set against the backdrop of the expulsion and dispersion. The heroine, Evangeline, remained loyal to her beloved, grieving and longing for him, wandering the earth, looking for him. Finally, she found him, among those dying from pestilence. He was an old man. She cried out his name and he heard her and she knelt at his bedside as he died. She thanked God that she had finally found him. Where better to affirm love and undying loyalty and devotion than at Grand-Pré?

But why do elderly people and people with babies go there for inspiration? I think there are several parts to the answer. First, and perhaps foremost, the Acadian people have survived. They have lived through trauma and suffering, but, in the end, they triumphed. So Grand-Pré represents endurance and perseverance and the ability to overcome great pain and hardship.

Second, the history of the Acadians can never be entirely healed (How can you heal the horror of forced dispersion?), but the fact that it has been told by the people whose story it is and acknowledged by the descendants of the offenders is certainly healing. And the fact that the story is known by people around the world is a great balm.

Third, and very significant, is the fact that the Acadians refused to be kept down. Their spirit of joy, creativity, and vitality permeate the site. They faced devastation and came up battered but triumphant. Grand-Pré whispers to visitors that if the Acadians could do it, so can they.

People who go to Grand-Pré often say that the place is an affirmation of life. It refuses to give death the final say. The Acadians represent the strength of human will and the ability to bear and overcome tragedy. There is always hope—not some blind, romantic hope, but a concrete reality, as evidenced by the survival of a decimated people.

Couples can survive the difficulties of marriage. Babies can be fortified to endure the slings and arrows of life. Older people can be brave in the face of loss, disappointment, aging.

Above all, Grand-Pré communicates an authentic history, rather than one whitewashed or compromised to make it easier for visitors. It tells a terrible story, but the spirit of the courageous and enduring people who lived there has been allowed to remain. The site is restorative. Visitors learn how the Acadians worked in harmony with the land and transformed salt fields into fertile farmland. Anything can be transformed. Fields. Tragedy. Life itself. Anything seems possible.

For me, the Acadians' story is a human story. Any of us can be stricken, but we can rise again and flourish. And we can celebrate that: our own survival and the survival of people and groups of people around us. We can live through physical and emotional disasters, trauma, pogroms, diasporas. Not only can we survive, but we can thrive.

Grand-Pré reminded me of the importance of history. It's axiomatic that if we don't know and learn from history, we are doomed to repeat it. In a sense, we have different technologies from our human ancestors, but the emotions, moods, needs, wants, and errors of today are the same as they always were in the past. When I am walking and talking with a friend, I sometimes imagine for a moment that we are in ancient Rome, wearing togas, walking in the shadows of a temple, having the same conversation. I am sure that our human essence has not changed over time. People have always complained about their children, their leaders, their parents, their spouses, their work, repairing their homes. They triumphed and failed. History is about people as much as it is about events. I think that the more deeply we penetrate history, the more we understand both.

Some folks learn history from books, others from TV or the Internet. Sometimes it comes through the oral tradition and is passed down in stories and legends. To me, the most powerful and direct way to get involved with history is through travel: wherever I go, I learn about the people who live there and where they came from. I learn all I can. I immerse myself in a culture and try to absorb and remember everything people say about their origins, ancestors, heroes and heroines, migration patterns, mistakes, triumphs, defeats, trading, leadership, allies, enemies, warmongering, peacemaking, challenges, and adaptations to the ebb and flow of existence. I listen because I am inspired by their history and mystery. I listen as though my survival depends upon it because I believe it does.

Every time I travel, every time I encounter people whose lives and cultures are different from mine, I am amazed at how their existence on this blue marble we call Earth adds depth, breadth, perspective, meaning, and joy to my own life.

About the Author

JUDITH FEIN is an award-winning international travel journalist who lives to leave. She resided for more than ten years in North Africa and Europe, where she ran an experimental theatre company and was an actor and director. She is an alumna of the Sundance Institute and worked as a film and television writer in Hollywood for twelve years. She has had ten plays produced in the U.S. and Europe, and one of her short plays has been performed around the world. She was the recipient of a grant from Opera America to create the libretto for the enthusiastically-reviewed opera "Hotel Eden" with composer Henry Mollicone.

Judith has a passion for adventures that are exotic, authentic, quirky, historic and immersed in local culture. She has written travel articles for more than ninety prominent magazines, newspapers and Internet sites. She was a regular reporter for "The Savvy Traveler" on public radio for six years, is Travel Editor of *Spirituality and Health* magazine, senior travel writer for the *San Diego Jewish Journal* and Contributing Writer for *Organic Spa* magazine. She is the editor and co-founder, with Ellen Barone, of the popular website http://www.YourLifeisaTrip.com. She is an acclaimed speaker for many venues and is known for her informational, humorous and inspirational talks on a wide variety of subjects. She is Vice President of the Travel Journalist Guild and a member of the Society of American Travel Writers. With her photojournalist husband

Paul Ross, she produces travel videos, slideshows and does travel performances. Judith and Paul teach travel writing and photography around the globe and sometimes invite friends and appealing strangers to come on trips with them.

Judith's website is: http://www.GlobalAdventure.us

Acknowledgements and Thanks

To Paul Ross, my husband, partner, soul mate, colleague, friend, editor, clown, teacher, support team, chef, masseur, photographer, videographer, voice-over coach, consoler, shrink, inspiration and man who schlepps the luggage.

To *Spirituality and Health* magazine, where I am the travel editor. Years ago, I was moaning about having such rich, soulful experiences with other cultures and how difficult it was to place stories about them. "You can write for us," said editor-in-chief Steve Kiesling. And he meant it.

To everyone I mentioned in the book for gracing me with their time, energy, insights, generosity, knowledge and open hearts. In the past year, Maori elder John Wilson, the High Priest of the ancient Israelite Samaritans and Paca from Sahagun passed away. May their good deeds on earth earn them a peaceful rest.

When one travels as much as I have, it's easy to feel disconnected and out-of-the-loop when one comes home. Over the years, having meaningful and long-lasting relationships has been extremely important to me. I want to thank my friends for understanding when I am too deluged to talk on the phone and switching over to email. Thanks for the parties, dinners, outings and invites that make us feel cared about and connected.

To Nancy King, who put down her own books to climb inside the soul of my book and offer me brilliant, inspired, generous and spot-on editorial advice.

To Jennifer Hanan for her powerful insights and above-and-beyond-the-call-of-friendship media help.

To Ellen Barone, my partner and co-founder of www.YourLifeisaTrip.com

To Andrew Adleman, who surprised us one day by providing us with www.GlobalAdventure.us, our website.

To my editor, Betsy Robinson, who approached the book with both head and heart.

To my publishers, specifically Victoria, Paul and Matt Sutherland, who committed to *Life Is A Trip* as soon as I gave them the manuscript.

To friends who have supported my flights of fancy, stayed in touch with me during my travels, kept the home fires burning and made me feel welcomed when I came home: Louise Rubin, Jade Gordon, Debbie Band, Judy Crawford, Devorah Leah and Berel Levertov, Brett Goldberg, Deb Finkelstein, all my Tuesday night buddies.

To friends who have traveled with us to exotic destinations: Judy Backenstow, Kitty Miller, Linda Lenhard, Maida Rubin, Jeremy Faust, Nancy and all our travel writing students.

To friends who welcomed us into their homes: Marla Frumkin + Peter Stelzer, Christine Wilson, Stacy and Todd Sabin, Bob Linden, Abe + Gulhis, Elyn Aviva and Gary White, Benny and Miriam Tsedaka, Ann and Oded Kleinberg, Marc Dupuis.

To my "twalking" (walking and talking) partners: Jennifer Hanan, Jean Ross, Mark Bradley, Susan Paradise, Jill Schwarz, Jan Eigner, Jim Terr, Bobby Mogill, Maura Studi, Erika Eckerstrand, Therese Williams, Paul White, Susan Berk, Linda Braun, Judy Herzl, Aysha Griffin, Jann Huizenga, Barb Alpert.

To much-appreciated cheerleaders: Jodie Rhodes, Maren Rudolph, Barbara and Tim Rogers, Marlan Warren, Wes Studi, Linda and Gary Storm, Diane Lobel, Artemes, Tone Forrest, John Rochester, Tony Grieco, Phil Hoffman.

To all my editors who gave me space, time and income.

To Ellen Valade, who started packing for me when we were in college.

To the Travel Journalists Guild, my travel writing colleagues and friends and the writers on www.YourLifeisaTrip.com

To my mother, Miriam Burstein, and my father, Edward Burstein, who instilled in me a life-long love for travel.

And to the world of friends I have yet to meet and travel with.

THE END

To all my editors who gave me space, time and income.

To Ellen Valade, who started packing for me when we were in college.

To the Travel Journalists Guild, my travel writing colleagues and friends and the writers on www.YourLifeisaTrip.com

To my mother, Miriam Burstein, and my father, Edward Burstein, who instilled in me a life-long love for travel.

And to the world of friends I have yet to meet and travel with.

THE END

Made in the USA
San Bernardino, CA
05 December 2014